"Tim Alba is a wordsmith with creative counsel for parents in successfully leading their children to become believers in Jesus Christ, and in maturing in their faith in a way that guides throughout their lives. These pages will excite you! They will enlighten you! They will enliven you on your parenting journey! Best of all, he will show you how to be sure that you realize the Lord is on this journey with you!"
—Jimmy Draper, President Emeritus of Lifeway Christian Resources

"Unlike parenting books that offer how-to's on potty training, homework habits, or videogame addiction, *Well Done* tackles the bigger parenting challenges: character, culture-faith conflicts, and personal accountability. Don't bother to read this book—unless you're serious about turning good intentions into permanent, positive outcomes for your kids and family!"
—Dianna Booher, Hall of Fame speaker and bestselling author of 49 books, including *Communicate Like a Leader* and *Communicate With Confidence*

"Well Done, Mom & Dad makes me want to be a better parent. I've read many books on parenting, but this one is unique. Vulnerable, personal and focused, it's what you get when you cross a strategic thinker like Tim with a passionate spiritual devotion to be a faithful parent. You'll want to read it all at once, but you'll want to keep it on the front of your desk for years of future reference. It's that valuable. And it's going to change the way you do parenting. Thank you, Tim, for this great resource!"
—John Meador, Lead Pastor of Cross City Church

"Tim Alba's *Well Done, Mom & Dad!* stirs an urgent and passionate desire to put his teachings into action! No matter how young or old your children are this is a spiritual compass that will impact each and every parent and child in an extraordinary way!"
—Joe Croce, CEO/Founder of CiCi's Pizza

Well Done, Mom & Dad!

A Practical Guide to Turn Good Intentions into Godly Legacies

Tim Alba

FaithHappenings Publishers

Centennial, Colorado

Printed in the United States of America

Scripture quotations are from *The New American Standard Bible*®. Copyright © The Lockman Foundation 1960, 1962, 1963, 1968, 1971, 1972, 1973, 1975, 1977, 1995, Used by permission.

For bulk orders, please contact the author at:

TimAlbaWD@gmail.com

FaithHappenings Publishing
A division of WordServe Literary
7500 E. Arapahoe Rd. Suite 285
Centennial, CO 80112
admin@wordserveliterary.com
303.471.6675

Cover Design: Evocative

Interior Book Design: Greg Johnson

Tim Alba (1962)

ISBN: 978-1-941555-47-7

Contents

As we begin, please ask yourself two questions:

1) Will my kids say . . .

"Mom, I rise up and bless you. Dad also praises you, saying: 'Many daughters have done nobly, but you excel them all.' Charm is deceitful and beauty is vain, but as a woman who fears the Lord, Mom, you shall be praised. Well done, Mom" (Proverbs 31:28-30 – personalized).

"Dad, you've directed me in the way of wisdom and led me in upright paths. When I walk, my steps won't be impeded; and if I run, I won't stumble. I've grabbed your instruction and not let go. I guard her, Dad, for she is my life. Well done, Dad" (Proverbs 4:11-13 – personalized).

2) Will my Lord say . . .

"You were faithful with a few things, I will put you in charge of many things; enter into the joy of your master. Well done, Mom and Dad" (Matthew 25:21– personalized).

Even if your kids don't yet praise your faithfulness, you can rest in this promise: God will. And if God says, "Well done, Mom" or "Well done, Dad," your kids will likely say it too one day.

A Reason for Real Hope

All Christian parents want happy, godly kids, but how do you turn those good intentions into a godly legacy? You may instruct kids well. You may even be a role model who lives it well. Still, do you ever struggle, wishing you knew the secret to making it happen?

That certainly was me as a young parent. I wanted to be a great dad. I even had a remarkable wife and parents. Still I struggled. Although my three kids – Leslie, Josh, and Caleb – were a blessing, they also had a challenging side, especially my baby girl, Leslie.

Like many kids, especially daughters, Leslie could wrap daddy around her little finger. Toddler Leslie would shout, "Daddy loooves Leslie! That's RIGHT!" Like no one else, she could melt my heart with a laugh, a song, or a hug. But Leslie had another knack. She could push my buttons. And heed my suggestions? Forget about it! Despite a deep relationship, Leslie and I clashed over attitudes, messy rooms, curfews, and, of course, boys.

I'll never forget the day fourteen-year-old Leslie invited a boy to our home. Let's call him Billy to protect the guilty. Like a good dad, I graciously issued no death threats to Billy. My shotgun, although loaded, sat anxiously unused. Rules were set. Principles clarified. And Billy arrived.

Did I sit between Leslie and Billy as they watched TV in the den? No. I stayed out of sight and made random trips to the fridge, which just happened to be next to the den. On my first two trips to the fridge, no problem. But on my third trip, I saw it . . . Leslie and Billy lip locked! Are you kidding me? It was all I could do to wait until the next day to lower the boom.

Leslie sauntered into the kitchen, avoiding eye contact, and grabbed the milk and a cup from the cupboard. Even the back of her head looked guilty.

I wasted no time. "Leslie Marie, what in the world were you thinking last night?!"

"What?" Her voice sounded like she was asking about the weather.

"No, Les. Don't even think about playing dumb. You know exactly what I'm talking about."

"Whaaaaaat?" She sat her drink down and gave me the look . . . the one where you know you're busted, but think you can fake your way out of it.

"Come on, Les. I saw you kissing Billy last night."

"Dad! You were spying on me?!" Big sigh, followed by an eye roll.

"Of course, I was checking on you. You're fourteen and I don't know this boy."

"But, Dad, it was nothing."

"Oh no, Les. I know what nothing looks like. And that was certainly not nothing. I know what boys that age have on their minds. I'm not saying Billy's a bad kid or that you crossed some terrible line. You know what I'm sayin'. You have to be more careful, Les. You can't trust boys."

Another, even bigger, eye roll. "Oh, Dad! You don't know boys!!!"

What does a dad – a grown boy – say to that? I didn't know whether to laugh or cry. I did wonder, though, how I'd failed as a parent. How many times could I tell her? How many ways? What would it take to sink in?

Back and forth we went, Leslie explaining why she was right (you know, the wisdom forged from fourteen years of learning all there is to know), and me guiding her back to reality. Today, it was smooching Billy. Tomorrow, it would be something else.

Leslie wasn't a bad kid. In fact, she was a great kid, except when we disagreed. And we disagreed often.

Ever been there? Surely you have, even though your specifics will vary, because of one reason: you're a parent. It comes with the territory. If you're not there now, strap on. It's coming. So what do you do when you can't see past today? When you're exhausted? When you're rebuffed because you can't possibly know anything? How could you, you're just a parent?!

While my wife, Anna, and I had many parenting challenges, we're here to tell you there's hope. No, there's no magic formula. But God does work. And kids can respond over time if you know the "secret" to helping kids be faithful. It's not telling them what to do or how to feel. You can't convince or force kids to be faithful. Instead, the secret is helping kids *want* to be faithful.

In this book, you'll read real-life stories, complete exercises, and create practical applications for one reason – to help your kids know how to be faithful . . . and want to. You'll learn how to lead through, not react to, parenting challenges. You'll find a reason for hope. Real hope. For in those times when you wonder if you've failed as a parent, you too can look forward to the day you get a priceless note, like this text from Leslie who had grown to be a godly woman:

> Dad, I just want to say how thankful I am for the grace you gave me. I know I never did things the easy or smartest way. You saw it and could have made me do better. I know I didn't listen a lot of the time and didn't honor your advice. But thank you for giving me so much grace, for loving and not shaming me when I came back to you, having failed, and asked for your help after the fact. I'm sure it was hard and frustrating to watch. But I see it now. I know now how well you loved me through the process. I'm thankful now to have experienced your good discipline as well as forgiveness and trust. I know I haven't always been the wisest, but I'm really grateful that you loved me anyway. Thanks, Dad!

Those are the nuggets of hope that struggling parents long for and wonder if they'll ever happen. But they *can* happen, even decades later, as you'll see in Chapters 6 and 12. You may be a young parent and think it's too early. You may have teenagers and think it's too late. Or you may be a grandparent trying to step in without overstepping. No matter your stage, the good news is that it's never too early or too late to prepare kids and grandkids to feel God's warm embrace.

Many exhausted parents think they'll do better when they get past a stage. But life only gets busier and harder. They say, "If only I could get through potty training." But just past potty training are training wheels. And after training wheels come training bras. And after training bras, it's drivers training. Today's drama becomes tomorrow's trauma unless you turn good intentions into a godly legacy. Thankfully, the solution isn't a secret. It's not complicated. It's a process – a dream and a plan called "well-done parenting" that any parent can apply over time to help their kids want to be faithful.

Well-done parenting not only prepares you to hear God say, "Well done." It also prepares kids to become godly parents. With vision, character, and culture, you can see eternal possibilities, not just today's problems. Let's begin exploring well-done parenting by imagining a scenario:

It's the dead of night and you're jolted awake with an uncontrollable cough. Screams pierce the stench and roar of raging fire as you run through suffocating smoke to a window. It's your family, safely outside, pleading for you to get out. Throwing open the bedroom door, you see there's time to grab only one thing before escaping. What do you grab?

Know this, what you'll grab is what you treasure. You won't weigh options or try to impress. Even if you don't know why, you'll grab what matters most at that moment. My wife said she'd grab her photo albums, but what would you grab?

In fact, we face this question daily. In the heat of the moment, we often don't grab the compelling treasures we wish we would. Instead, we grab convenient treasures – default choices that would never make a short list of priorities. How about you? Are you grabbing the faith and family you want to treasure, or are default choices grabbing you? For if you don't choose in advance, you easily forget why. And if you forget why, what kind of life (and perhaps eternity) waits for your family? But you don't have to wait for a tragedy to choose.

The tragedy is to not choose and live with the consequences. Then again, failing to choose is choosing to fail. How might your family be living with the consequences of your default choices? What do they need from you to turn those default choices into compelling treasures? Chances are, your family, like mine, needs a guide – simple tools to inspire and instruct, along with practical ways to understand why we sometimes fall short. Knowing how starts with knowing yourself.

Two kinds of Christian parents
Parents need to look beyond today's challenges to see tomorrow's champions. For indeed Leslie did eventually learn to not trust boys. It just took time and patience. And while Leslie had to make some tough choices, so did I. I had to learn about two kinds of Christian parents and decide which one I would be. How about you? Are you more like Parent A or Parent B?

Parent A	Parent B
Breaks habits	Bonds hearts
Fixes behavior	Funnels beliefs
Stops drama	Shapes dreams

Most parents are like Parent A, trying hard to break little Suzie's bad habits, fix her behavior, and stop her drama. They're not bad parents. They're good parents with good intentions, who

5

want simple solutions and quick fixes to break, fix, and stop today's problems. That's **default parenting** – the well-intended choices that get you through another hectic day. But well intended is not well done. We've all been there, but we don't have to stay there. We can become more like Parent B.

Parent B sees little Suzie differently – as the godly adult she can become. These parents also break Suzie's habits, but they do so by bonding with her heart. They fix her behavior by funneling her beliefs. And they stop her drama by shaping her dreams. They don't make Suzie's choices; they make it easy for her to choose well. That's **well-done parenting** – turning well-intended choices into children who hear God say, "Well done!"

Default parents allow default kids to happen. Well-done parents, though, bond with kids in ways they can hardly resist.

In *Families and Faith: How Religion is Passed Down across Generations*, Vern Bengtson researches why some families pass down their faith, while others don't. His conclusion after tracking 350 families for four decades: faith legacies continue most when children bond emotionally with their parents, especially their fathers. Despite vast societal changes, these "bonded" kids are more likely to continue their families' faith than leave it.

Armed with that hope, this book prepares families for a heavenly reunion. You'll learn practical *ways* of bonding with personal *whys*. Your dreams – perhaps God's dreams – can live on through your kids by embracing the three bonds of well-done parenting.

Bond #1: Vision

The first bond of well-done parenting is compelling vision that sees how to turn what *is* into what *can be*. In Chapters 1 to 5, you'll choose your treasures using 50-20-5-1 Embrace – a simple exercise that prepares your family for heavenly embraces by embracing your compelling treasures.

50-20-5-1 Embrace

50 Pursuits

20 Priorities

5 Passions

1 Purpose

"Well done!"

You'll choose fifty pursuits that matter, which you'll narrow to twenty priorities that matter most, then five passions you'll live for, and finally one purpose you won't live without. Families, co-workers, and friends have all used this tool to discover compelling vision. A mom said, "This is important enough that I want my family to know their treasures and learn this as children." A friend said, "It's a roadmap to my future. It changed how I spent last weekend with my grandkids. We did things together that really matter to me. And that changes everything."

After shaping a family vision, Chapter 6 provides practical tips to make it come alive. You'll learn six ways to visualize a family vision that inspires your kids to do the same one day.

Bond #2: Character

The second bond of well-done parenting is timeless character – living your chosen qualities with integrity. In Chapters 7 to 11, the 1-2-3-U Discovery assessment helps you lead yourself well in order to lead your family well. It's a progression of character that puts your family on the path to faithfulness.

1-2-3-U Discovery

While books abound on topics like success, significance, and legacies, this book reveals their interdependence . . . how fulfilling treasures birth success, success becomes significance, and significance grows into faithful legacies. Like this pyramid, though, life plateaus unless others, not you (U), are on top.

Faithful family legacies are forged in character that connects kids with parents. Thus, Chapter 12 shows you how to meld a secret sauce of character qualities that kids want for themselves.

Bond #3: Culture

The third bond crafts a captivating family culture that multiplies your values through an inspiring environment of faithfulness. You'll learn how to prepare kids to be purposefully courageous and passionately contagious. In Chapter 13, you'll learn how to make unique family promises. Chapter 14 reveals how to create memory tattoos that kids can't forget and wouldn't want to. And Chapter 15 prepares them for two kinds of heavenly hugs.

Vision invigorates. Character validates. Culture demonstrates. Vision opens kids' imaginations to see who God created them to be. Character makes vision believable and attainable. Culture adds authenticity so that kids want a godly legacy too.

Although Anna and I planned and tried hard, we missed the mark for years. We made plans to get married, find jobs, and buy a house. We even made plans for having kids. But we had no plan for parenting, and that had to change. This book shows you how with a dream and a plan.

Bill Yancey says: "A dream without a plan is just hope. And hope is not a strategy." I pray that you too will find a reason for real hope with your own compelling dream and practical plan. And not just any ol' dream . . . God's dream for your family:

> Make it *your* mission
> to make it *their* mission
> to hear God say, "Well done!"

Whatever your dream may be, I'll help you articulate it, live it, and engage your family in it. Then your kids can be eager and able to do the same for their own families one day. For what could be greater than having your kids run to you in heaven, squeeze you close, and say, "Well done, Mom and Dad"? That's the moment your dreams have come true. You've done your job. You've put faithfulness on a tee so your kids can whack it. You haven't tried to make them faithful. You've made it easy for them to know how . . . and *want* to.

You're more than well intended.

You've done well!

VISION

(CHOOSE YOUR TREASURES)

"Choose for yourself today whom you will serve . . . but as for me and my house, we will serve the Lord" (Joshua 24:15).

"Protect, through the Holy Spirit who dwells in us, the treasure which has been entrusted to you" (2 Timothy 1:14).

Chapter 1

50-20-5-1 Embrace

Have you ever pictured what it will be like when you take your first steps into heaven? The vision of that moment is likely as different as each person holding this book. Let me tell you mine.

My eyes are opening from a fog as I ponder the stories of my life. My chest is actually pounding, and waves of emotions engulf me. It's as if a cloudy veil has suddenly and completely been lifted.

For the first time, I can look back and see my life with perfect clarity. Struggles, so hard to explain at the time, had been interlocking pieces of a grand puzzle. People, even those long-since forgotten, are hugging me. As it turns out, my seemingly random acts of kindness had been providential pieces of their life stories. Shamefully, I can also see something else – opportunities lost. All this would be surreal if it wasn't so surely real.

I'm standing there in awe, soaking it all in. And then it happens.

I look up, see Jesus, and feel inexpressible joy and reverence. It's what I believed would happen, yet it's far more glorious than I could have ever imagined. Instinctively, I drop to my knees and fall face first to the ground as my Lord runs from His throne with the most captivating, loving grin.

As Jesus lifts me up and cradles my head to His chest, He whispers in my ear, "Tim, I've been waiting for you soooo long!" I desperately want to shout or praise or say something worthy, but I'm utterly speechless. All I can do is rest in His arms and feel His warm embrace.

Looking piercingly into my tear-filled eyes, He says, "Welcome home, Tim!" And with a subtle nod and a few tears of His own, He utters these intimate words, "Thank you for making it easy for your family to love me too! Well done, Dad!"

That's my vision, my personal dream. I want my wife and kids to say, "Well done, Dad," but nothing matters more to me than hearing it from my Lord. It's the reward for living well and the reason to do so. In recent years, though, God has given me a far grander dream. It's a family dream – a family vision – that grips my soul and drives me to help other families.

That grand dream is to watch Jesus do the same with *my kids*!

I can see the tears streaming down my kids' cheeks as they hug Jesus. I can feel their utter joy. I can sense their overwhelming peace. After embracing Jesus, they rise and run to me, throw their arms around me, and we embrace. Forever. Together. Every struggle, every life stage, every challenge we navigated . . . each one is now worth it all. We're safely home.

Now, imagine that moment with *your* family.

If only you could force this to happen or make kids want your dreams. But you can't. They have to want their own. Even great parenting doesn't guarantee it. You can make it far more likely, though, by instilling a compelling family vision that sees what is and what can be for your family.

Some parents see only what they want their kids to be. Others see only today's reality. Compelling vision sees both – what is and what can be. In Chapters 2 and 3, you'll consider the reality of who you and your kids are and what you treasure. Chapters 4 and 5 help you decide who you want to be and what you will treasure.

Compelling family visions start with compelling parents. Compelling parents don't glance. They gaze. They discern. They dream big and look ahead. It's hard to raise kids to become godly parents, though, unless you first envision what you want for them. And it's hard to envision what you want for them until you come to grips with how you've been parenting. Here are two questions to help you see what kind of parent you have been.

1) How were you raised? Chances are, how you were raised is how you are parenting. It's comfortable for you, but is it compelling for your kids? Likely not. If you struggled with parents who raised you this way, no wonder your kids struggle with you.

2) Are you the parent you prefer to be, or the parent your kids need you to be? Initially, I raised my kids the way I preferred – how I was raised. Then I realized my kids need something different. They need me to connect with how *they* are wired and lead them to want godly treasures that connect with them.

For example, as a young dad, I was strong and stoic because that's what dads do, right? Not necessarily. That was my default because it's how my dad did it. My kids needed a strong dad, but as explained later in this chapter, they also needed qualities like vulnerability. If I'd listed qualities of great dads, vulnerability wouldn't have cracked the top 100. It never crossed my mind. But since my child needs it, I'm learning to be vulnerable.

Your treasures aren't necessarily your kids' treasures. Each child is unique, so each child needs unique attention. What drains one child can compel another to new heights. To one, it's just a familiar what, but to another, it's a compelling why. Your job isn't to get your children to copy you. It's to align their godly treasures with God who gives them those treasures.

To compel is to grab your attention, causing you to believe and act. Thus, compelling parents cast a vision that is attention grabbing, convincing, and intentional. As Michelle Anthony says

15

in *Spiritual Parenting*, this "is not perfect parenting – it's parenting from a spiritual perspective with eternity in mind." It's helping kids discover how they're wired and who they want to be, so that they'll discover godly treasures too.

Who do you know with compelling vision? Let me introduce you to two people whose vision shaped mine – Lynda Bethea and Grandpa Loyd.

A missional missionary
On March 27, 1991, while driving on a rural Kenyan road to pick up their children, Lynda and Ralph Bethea saw a man lying on the road. Rather than passing by, as warned by fellow missionaries, they stopped to help.

The man in the road and three hidden thieves attacked Ralph with iron pipes and machetes. Instinctively, Lynda ran to Ralph's aid because she loved him and would lay down her life for his. With all their fury, the thieves turned on Lynda until she could fight no more. As Ralph crawled to Lynda and clutched her brutalized body, she said four final phrases that still stir my soul:

> Don't hate these men. They need Jesus.
> Take care of the children, all the children.
> I love you.
> I'm going home.

How could Lynda seek redemption, not revenge? How could she live her last moments in horror, yet die in peace? Going home, not fearing the unknown? It's simple. Lynda's life, like her death, reflected how she saw people, especially the One who mattered most to her – Jesus.

Jesus forgave His killers, just like Lynda. As Jesus died, He asked for the care of His family, as did Lynda. Jesus loved until His last breath, and so did Lynda. Jesus commended His spirit into God's hand and went home, similar to Lynda. For when you live like Jesus, you can die like Him.

We likely won't die like Lynda, but we can live like her. We can inspire others and experience God's well-done embrace. Lynda's life testifies that our treasures are utterly worth it when *what* matters most is based on *who* matters most. Her vision helps me embrace my own, as did the servant whose name I carry as my middle name – Grandpa Loyd.

A grand grandpa

I loved Grandpa Loyd's silly stories, fishing trips, and nightly bowls of ice cream. What a great guy. After he died, though, I discovered his secret. While relatives took furniture and keepsakes, my mom gave me something that reveals Grandpa Loyd's heart – his Bible.

I now know his favorite verses, which were worn and underlined. I know his passion for salvation and his favorite devotions. Through his Bible, I see why the man whose name I carry was a devoted servant with compelling vision. It helps me love him even more. And it makes me wonder: What stories does my Bible tell about me?

Grandpa Loyd modeled how to guard entrusted treasures (2 Timothy 1:14). And his daughter showed me how to love and follow Christ, whose name I also carry – a Christian. But we can't copy Grandpa Loyd's or Lynda's vision. God gives us our own vision to fulfill.

My kids and I know ours.

Do your kids and you know yours?

You can if you'll pursue it like a hidden treasure (Proverbs 2:1-5). Your kids can be more than happy kids or godly kids. They can become godly adults who, in turn, help their own kids want to be faithful.

Every parent casts some form of vision. But is yours a default vision, or a vision your kids need? Yes, a compelling family vision is a big dream, but God is in the big dream business. And He'll use virtually anything to get us to dream big. For me, He used two tornados.

Two tornados. One life lesson.

Alarms blared, skies blackened, and blustery winds became eerily silent. "If you're in the path of the tornado, seek shelter immediately," warned the TV weatherman. My parents grabbed us kids, ran to the basement, and prayed. Rains flooded fields, pigs blew across the sky, and homes disappeared. Although I saw God's protection, I also saw how my parents' choices on that day reflected their daily lives. In the storm, they grabbed the same two things they grabbed every day – their faith and family.

Twenty-five years later, another tornado threatened, except this time I was the dad. Anna couldn't leave her building, so she frantically called me to go home. When I arrived, the house was fine, but my kids were nowhere. I searched and searched. I yelled their names. No reply. Finally, I found them, crammed into a tiny bathroom. I'll never forget what I saw when I opened that door. They were having a party! Music was playing. Kids were laughing. The dog was frolicking. So I did what any good dad would do, I joined in. We ate pizza and watched the tornado movie, *Twister*. Turns out, Anna had called and told the kids to grab only what they needed, get inside that bathroom, and shut the door.

On that day, I learned an enduring life lesson – that kids, like adults, grab what they treasure. My thirteen-year-old grabbed her stereo and makeup. Makeup, really? She became a fashion designer who loves to sing. My eleven-year-old wanted music too but big sis was in charge of tunes, so he took a Bible and a flashlight. He's now a godly musician and a light to others. My eight-year-old grabbed his video game and dog. Yep, he's a graphic designer and dog owner. I didn't have to teach them to grab what they treasure. They just knew. And so do you. But are you grabbing the best treasures?

Despite good intentions, the best treasures get squeezed out. We don't know how this happens, but it happens until we do one thing – we choose. Why? Because our time, money, and efforts go where our heart is, and our heart goes where our treasure is (Luke 12:34). So, let's fill our life funnels with treasures based on a family vision of our choosing.

The choices filling our lives are like sealed containers taken to high altitudes. They burst under pressure, revealing what's inside. Sometimes, we're pleasantly surprised; often, not. But the real you was, is, and always will be the product of your daily choices. Nothing more. Nothing less.

For example, I can't exercise away bad food choices. I'll have love handles on my hips as long as I want chips to be their own food group. Good food causes good health. Bad food, bad health.

If flesh pours in, then impurity, hatred, and jealousy pour out. But if the Spirit pours in, then love, joy, and peace overflow (Galatians 5:19-23). What flows in will flow out. Thus, we must guard what flows into us because it will flow into our family.

That's what the 50-20-5-1 Embrace exercise does. It reveals what's flowing into your life so that you change what flows out. It helps parents cast a family vision by discovering what each family member truly treasures. And by embracing a grand family vision, you'll prepare your family for God's grand embrace.

50-20-5-1 Embrace

The 50-20-20-1 Embrace exercise unpacks each person's vision at today's stage of life. It's simple. You select **Fifty Pursuits** that make you happy, which you narrow down to **Twenty Priorities** that you sacrifice to enjoy, then **Five Passions** that fulfill you, and **One Purpose** that causes you to feel God's embrace. The key isn't the list; it's what the process reveals. For example, in doing this exercise as a family, I learned that my teenage son, Caleb, needs vulnerability. Here was his feedback:

> I really enjoyed doing this as a family. I learned so much about our family and what they deem most important. It was cool seeing personalities shine through their lists. The process forces you to evaluate where you are in life and areas to improve. I can definitely see doing this with my future family. I especially liked the vulnerability, which was crucial for real penetration to occur. The list highlights the importance of the end result and how you must change today in order to reach that end result.

The benefits of doing this exercise as a family are similar to what Larry Osborne describes in his book *Sticky Teams*: "Working through the ideas and principles together has far more value than the actual information shared. It creates a shared pool of information and experiences that puts everyone on the same page." And, oh my, what countless hurting families would give to have their kids on the same page!

In the first bond of well-done parenting – vision to choose your treasures – you'll discover a compelling why and compelling way to get your family on the same page. Pursuing that vision, however, isn't a stroll. It's a race with a prize (1 Corinthians 9:24-26, Philippians 3:13-14). This race, though, has a twist.

Unlike Olympians who compete against others, we're *completing* others. It's not even about finishing first; it's about together finishing strong. In fact, our race is more like the Special Olympics. While Special Olympians are incredible athletes, many of them strive for a prize greater than fanfare – a loving embrace at the finish line. They give their best to make loved ones proud. Even if you're not gifted, you can make your Heavenly Father proud by running to Him and finishing strong.

In Chapters 2 through 5, the 50-20-5-1 Embrace exercise unpacks each person's treasures. Then in Chapter 6, you'll learn six practical, visual ways to turn individual family member's treasures into a compelling family vision. You'll learn how to lead your family to *want* a godly future and *how* to make it happen.

For kids to see a new future, though, they need to see us lead the way. Will we choose our preferences or what they need? Will we pursue whats (habits and behaviors) or whys (hearts and beliefs)? In *Shepherding a Child's Heart*, Tedd Tripp says we "worry more about the 'what' of behavior than the 'why.' Accordingly, (we) spend an enormous amount of energy in controlling and constraining behavior. To the degree and extent to which our focus is on behavior, we miss the heart."

What are you pouring into your kids' life funnels? Behaviors or beliefs? Habits or hearts? Whatever it is, please don't wait for a tragedy before choosing what's worth grabbing and pouring into your kids. Moving kids from well-intended to well-done requires vision. I've shared the vision I'm pouring into my family. In the next chapter, you'll take your first step – Fifty Pursuits – in pouring a compelling vision into *your family*.

More than just questions to discuss, here are questions to help you make choices that you'll actually practice with your family.

Choices to practice:

1. What do you imagine it will be like to enter heaven?

2. Are you the parent you prefer to be or the parent your kids need you to be? How could you be the parent they need?

3. Who shaped your family's legacy? How did they do this?

Chapter 2

Fifty Pursuits

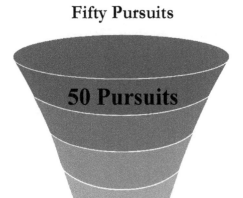

Fifty-six men, each risking everything to pursue a common vision, signed a document declaring their choices. This declaration defined their treasures, upon which a visionary country was born in 1776:

> We hold these truths to be self-evident, that all men are created equal, that they are endowed by their Creator with certain unalienable Rights, that among these are Life, Liberty, and the pursuit of Happiness.

Praise God for endowing these rights, but please don't miss what they are: life, liberty, and pursuits. Not happiness; it's the pursuit of happiness. Happiness wasn't guaranteed, but they wouldn't live without pursuing it. Without declared pursuits, these fifty-six founding fathers would have been *floundering* fathers

– good ideas without chosen ideals. They decided which pursuits were worth dying for, so we remember what they lived for.

In fact, every parent can be a founding father or founding mother of a godly legacy. Your life is a declaration to your kids of what matters to you, and your pursuits are a bold "John Hancock" that shapes their hopes and dreams. But is your life declaring a vision you want your kids to emulate?

Even if your pursuits aren't written in a document, they're etched in your family. Like a funnel, they pour out of your life and into your kids. So if you want godliness to flow from your kids, let them first see it flow from you. They may not be able to explain it yet, but they'll never forget it and one day they'll likely want to do the same.

For example, how did Joshua have faith to conquer the Promised Land? It's because Moses first poured faith into Joshua's funnel. Therefore, decades later, Joshua could say: "Choose for yourselves today whom you will serve … but as for me and my house, we will serve the Lord" (Joshua 24:15).

What flows out of your life are the pursuits that make you happy enough to allow in. If you were to list your favorite pursuits, what would it include? That's the first step of 50-20-5-1 – writing a list of fifty things that matter to you called "Fifty Pursuits."

Have you ever taken time, even half an hour, to write what matters to you? I lived over 430,000 hours before doing so. These aren't fifty things that you want to start doing. They're fifty things that already make you happy, big or small, like relationships, memories, milestones, work, values, food, animals, music, events, health, necessities, hobbies, and more.

There's something about writing them down that makes you reconsider what you're actually pursuing. Then again, you don't have to be John Hancock or Joshua to pursue your treasures. Anyone can pursue them, including *your* family.

At the end of Chapter 5 is the 50-20-5-1 form to write your Fifty Pursuits, along with 100 generalized examples from our seminar attendees that you can personalize for you. For example, instead of a general word like Family, use names. Instead of Career, my musician son wrote "win a Grammy." Some people have been hesitant or concerned that their lists weren't good enough, but please don't worry about that. It's great as long as it reflects the uniqueness of you.

Creating Fifty Pursuits has two simple instructions:
1. Write fifty answers to: "I'm happy when enjoying . . ."
2. Use short answers (one to three words, when possible).

What happens to your list, though, when life changes . . . when you graduate, start a family, change careers, raise teenagers, care for aging parents, or battle health problems? The answer is: your pursuits change. In Luke 17:12-19, ten lepers pursued healing. Once healed, nine of them crossed healing off their lists and moved on, neglecting their Savior. While it's natural for pursuits to change, keep relishing transforming pursuits and releasing trivial pursuits. For illustration purposes, here were my pursuits when I began writing this book.

Fifty Pursuits that matter ("I'm happy when enjoying. . .")

1. God says, "Well done!"	2. Purpose & Passion
3. A faithful legacy	4. My kids saying I'm godly & their hero
5. Integrity when no one is watching	6. Heavenly treasures to lay at His feet
7. Anna's embrace	8. Loving Anna
9. Compelling "whys"	10. God's anointing
11. Content, not satisfied	12. Serving others
13. Providing for family	14. Mom's enchiladas
15. Choosing wisely	16. "Nuggets" of hope
17. Earning respect	18. Writing my book
19. Touching your soul	20. Good judgment

21. Persistence
22. Making Dad proud
23. True friendship
24. Excellence
25. Surrendering to God
26. Using unique gifts
27. "Shameless" praise
28. Answered prayers
29. Purposeful paintings
30. Family's laughter
31. Pondering my Bible
32. Balance
33. Great music (loud)
34. Proactively change
35. Hot showers
36. Exploring/traveling
37. Tenacious work ethic
38. Historical churches
39. CiCi's Pizza
40. Executing plans
41. Hawkeye football
42. Him-dependence
43. Bearing fruit
44. Health & Exercise
45. Always learning
46. Defending freedom
47. Solving problems
48. Real leadership
49. Never forgetting why
50. Finishing strong

One of the best ways to use these lists is telling the stories behind them. For example, my kids loved learning how Hawkeye football (#41) reflects undaunted loyalty, Balance (#32) is a quest for joy while maximizing potential, and Mom's enchiladas (#14) signify my mom's love for me. Each pursuit is an interlocking puzzle piece of my life story. (In Chapter 14, you'll learn how to share the stories behind your list.)

Over the next three chapters, you'll refine your list, which will refine you. In leading my family to complete the 50-20-5-1 exercise, I had to rethink my own treasures. And the verdict? Hands down, it was one of the most bonding family experiences of my life! It changed our pursuits by changing our perspectives.

My family saw each other differently. With both common patterns and unique threads, it was a litmus test of what was soaking deep inside them. My kids not only caught a glimpse of the heritage they had been receiving, they also began choosing a heritage for their future families. Here's how it starts.

Laying a family foundation – Session #1

I suggest at least two sessions for this exercise. In Session #1, everyone writes Fifty Pursuits. You can provide the 100 pursuits at the end of Chapter 5 and give them thirty minutes to start. (They'll refine their lists later anyway.) After reading aloud their Fifty Pursuits, everyone shares something they learned about each other. (The next chapter describes the latter half of Session #1.)

If possible, however, add a step – write Fifty Pursuits before Session #1. For example, I took my family to a new restaurant, introduced the idea, gave examples, and asked them to bring their Fifty Pursuits to Session #1. When you do, share your heart. Be transparent. Create intrigue. Explain why you're doing this together and what you want *for them*.

There's no bad time to do 50-20-5-1. Some parents have asked, "But what if my kids are preschoolers?" That's a great time because new parents want better for their kids and are eager to do so. Some parents of preteens and teenagers wonder if it's too late. Those parents are often the most surprised, because they hear their kids open up and even praise each other's treasures. Then again, how often does your family share why you admire each other? Never, right? Well, it can with this exercise.

Another common surprise is the commonality and uniqueness of family members' lists. What common items would you expect in your family's lists? What uniquenesses? Here's my son's Top 50 when he was 17 years old. (And, no, he didn't follow my instructions to use one- to three-word answers.)

Fifty things that matter to Caleb

1. Love of family	2. Respect of parents
3. Time with mother	4. Making your father proud
5. Grandma's enchiladas	6. Grandmama's jambalaya
7. Mom's pizza	8. Health & fitness
9. Seeking truth	10. Honor

11. Respect

12. Humility

13. Patience

14. Selflessness

15. Joy in small things

16. Surrounded with good influences

17. Learning from your past

18. Serving God in any circumstance

19. Missions

20. Share your testimony

21. Consistent prayer

22. Countless blessings

23. Time in the Word

24. Music

25. Making wise choices

26. Accountability

27. Discipleship

28. Giving time where needed

29. Friends who bear the fruit they claim

30. Taking responsibility for your actions

31. Guard your heart/eyes

32. Memorize scripture

33. Making the most of what you have

34. Never forgetting your encounter at the cross

35. Fellowshipping with believers and others

36. Finding joy in Jesus, not in situation

37. Having a mentor

38. Being a mentor

39. Spending time wisely

40. Faithful in small things

41. See the bigger picture

42. Proactive in church

43. Family memories

44. Seeing past yourself

45. Fighting enemies with love

46. Loosely holding on to your possessions

47. Surrender

48. Sacrifice

49. Admitting failure

50. Praising Him in storms

The shocker to me was that nearly half of Caleb's pursuits were similar to mine, even though he hadn't seen my list! For example, we both had my mom's enchiladas, wise choices, and making your father proud. Others were different views of common family values, such as my #49: "Never forgetting why" and Caleb's #34: "Never forgetting your encounter at the cross."

It's also fun discovering everyone's uniqueness. I've seen parents joyfully cry over their kids' values, co-workers pray for exposed problems, and a husband surprised by his wife's desire to adopt. Hearts break and melt at the same time. Imagine what bonding memories your family could make by creating and sharing your lists. Here's what my son Josh said:

> It makes you think about yourself, and it helps you understand where your family is coming from. We don't always share what matters most with each other. We can usually tell some of the things just by watching each other's lives, but talking about it is a great way to self-discovery as well as communal discovery.

No matter your age or stage, 50-20-5-1 works. You don't have to be John Hancock who changed the world by boldly declaring his pursuits. You just need to change *your* world by boldly pursuing one choice, one child, one marriage, one friend at a time.

Rather than struggling with the consequences of a default legacy, you can pursue a legacy of your choosing. As you'll discover in the next three chapters, by progressively narrowing your Fifty Pursuits down to compelling treasures, you'll help your family choose their own.

If you will, you'll never be the same.

And neither will they.

Choices to practice:

1. What needs to stop flowing into your life funnel?

2. What common and unique pursuits do you expect in your family members' Top 50 lists?

3. Which of your Fifty Pursuits would most surprise your kids?

Note: You can also access a free Workbook to help you complete this book's various exercises, including 50-20-5-1, at www.timalba .com. Use it to guide your family and friends to join you in the pursuit of hearing, "Well done!" from God and family.

Chapter 3

Twenty Priorities

Paul Kimball was livin' the dream. Family, job, house, money, influence, everything society says we should pursue. The most impressive thing about Paul, though, wasn't his success; it was his priorities. Paul prioritized obedience over worldly pursuits.

At the height of Paul's career, God gave Paul a new dream – to teach at John Brown University. By joyfully obeying God's call, this humble legacy maker molded the dreams of thousands of future leaders like me. Paul didn't just teach us knowledge, he taught us how to leave a legacy. Legacy makers like Paul refine their pursuits into priorities using three priority primers available to us all: 1) sacrifice, 2) desperation, and 3) dependence.

Primer #1: Sacrifice
Legacy makers like Paul not only prioritize what matters most, but also lay aside lesser pursuits. They thrive with less so that others can experience more. Then again, the proof of what

matters most isn't the dream you'll pursue to be happy. It's the dream you'll sacrifice to be faithful.

Prioritizing is harder than pursuing because it has to sacrifice good pursuits. The problem is that pursuits build up over time and dilute your calling. Like refinishing furniture, legacy makers strip away the old build up before applying a fresh new finish. Adding layers is easier than stripping away, but ease isn't on a legacy maker's short list of priorities. Sacrifice is.

Sacrifice is refreshing because it's selfless and liberating. It enables great by setting aside good. If your kids named someone who sacrifices, expecting nothing in return, would they pick you? Sacrifice is even more impactful with the second priority primer of legacy makers – desperation.

Primer #2: Desperation

Legacy makers know the joy of desperation that forges life-changing priorities amidst the smallest trials. For example, we had driven 1,100 miles in a clunky van to Orlando with three young kids who alternated between laughter and death threats. It was pitch dark, but I knew exactly where our hotel was located . . . because I saw it on my left after missing my exit. In frustration, I turned around and drove back, but missed it again. "Blast it! Stupid hotel," I barked and punched the steering wheel as we passed the hotel on my right.

The kids sat in stunned silence, watching me lose it. Like a typical man, I refused to stop for directions. Instead, I turned around, even more determined to not repeat my mistake. And a few minutes later, I yet again saw the hotel . . . on my left as I passed it a third time. Seriously?! This was getting ridiculous. I kept driving in stern silence until my kids broke loose in laughter, waving wildly and shouting, "Bye-bye, hotel. Bye-bye!"

I knew where I wanted to go, but assumed I could get there myself. Pride had become a higher priority than humility. We've all been there, but legacy makers don't camp there. With a selfless desperation for their priorities, they turn lapses into lessons, ready to live the third priority primer – dependence.

Primer #3: Dependence

For much of life, we strive for independence. My toddler daughter Leslie would pooch out her little lip and defiantly declare, "I can do it *myself!*" News flash, no she couldn't. She was dependent and didn't know it. Adults, too, live with a mirage of independence. We may not pooch out our lip, but we often mistakenly think we can do it ourselves.

Upon what do you depend? Love, for a sense of worth? Money, for security? Success, for hope? While I want love, money, and success, relying on them is a way of pooching out my lip and telling God, "I can do it myself." News flash, no I can't. No one can. But God can. He must depend on Him every day.

Family legacies are also forged by depending on our diversities. For example, Anna is creative; I'm analytical. She's a party waiting to happen; I party after completing my to-do list. She helps me enjoy the journey; I help her envision a joyous destination. Our opposites are many, but we depend on two priorities to complete our relationship – faith and family.

Legacy makers let priorities complement, not compete. When priorities compete, families fight. But when they complement, kids learn that love and respect are offerings, not obligations, enabling them to truly love and respect God, as did Leslie. No longer an "I can do it *myself*" toddler, Leslie is now a devoted mom dependent on God. Until she created a 50-20-5-1 vision, though, Leslie didn't truly know her priorities because she never had a forum to choose them. And neither had I.

This is where 50-20-5-1 gets intriguing, as you carve your Fifty Pursuits that matter down to Twenty Priorities that matter *most* – what you are sacrificing for, desperate for, and depending on. These aren't twenty things you want to matter most. They're what already does matter most to you.

Again using the 50-20-5-1 form at the end of Chapter 5 or the free Workbook at www.timalba.com, circle twenty of your Fifty Pursuits that best answer: "I sacrifice to enjoy . . ." Then take a few minutes to write those Twenty Priorities in the 50-20-5-1 form. For example, here's how my Fifty Pursuits became Twenty Priorities.

Tim's 50-20-5-1 Embrace

Fifty Pursuits that matter ("I'm happy when enjoying. . .")

1 God says, "Well done!"	2 Purpose & Passion	3 A faithful legacy
4 My kids say I'm godly & their hero	5 Integrity when no one is there to watch	6 Heavenly treasures to lay at His feet
7 Anna's embrace	8 Loving Anna	9 Compelling "whys"
10 God's anointing	11 Content, not satisfied	12 Serving others
13 Providing for family	14 Mom's enchiladas	15 Choosing wisely
16 "Nuggets" of hope	17 Earning respect	18 Writing my book
19 Touching your soul	20 Good judgment	21 Persistence
22 Making Dad proud	23 True friendship	24 Excellence
25 Surrendering to God	26 Using unique gifts	27 "Shameless" praise
28 Answered prayers	29 Purposeful paintings	30 Family's laughter
31 Pondering my Bible	32 Balance	33 Great music (loud)
34 Proactively change	35 Hot showers	36 Exploring/traveling
37 Tenacious work ethic	38 Historical churches	39 CiCi's Pizza
40 Executing plans	41 Hawkeye football	42 Him-dependence
43 Bearing fruit	44 Health & Exercise	45 Always learning
46 Defending freedom	47 Solving problems	48 Real leadership
49 Never forgetting why	50 Finishing strong	

Twenty Priorities that matter most ("I sacrifice to enjoy . . .")

1 God says, "Well done!"	2 Purpose & Passion	3 A faithful legacy
4 My kids say I'm godly & their hero	5 Integrity when no one is there to watch	6 Heavenly treasures to lay at His feet
7 Touching your soul	8 Pondering my Bible	9 God's anointing
10 Him-dependence	11 Excellence	12 Serving others
13 Providing for family	14 Writing my book	15 Choosing wisely
16 Earning respect	17 Balance	18 Loving Anna
19 Bearing fruit	20 Never forgetting why	

A common question is: But what if I have a priority that isn't in my Top 50? You can change your Top 50, but that doesn't answer how something can be in your Top 20 and not be in your Top 50. Maybe that priority isn't really a priority yet. You want it to be a priority, but is it even getting into your life funnel? Either way, don't overthink it. I had to change my Top 50 a few times after thinking through my Top 20 too.

Prioritizing is key because we can't juggle fifty priorities. We simply can't do it all. We try, but sadly the most important priorities often get dropped, while the urgent or easy ones continue. Less is more with life funnels because true joy comes from pursing the relative few priorities that matter most, not the many pursuits that make us happy.

Just remember that Fifty Pursuits and Twenty Priorities are about what actually does matter most to you – what is. (In the next chapter, we'll transition to what you want to matter most – what can be.) Below is an overview of the second half of Session #1, where families not only hope for a better legacy, they also begin birthing it.

Birthing a family legacy – Session #1 continues

After everyone reads their Fifty Pursuits and shares what they learned about each other, Session #1 continues by having them circle Twenty Priorities, share them, and explain why they picked their priorities. End by asking them to come to Session #2, having narrowed their Twenty Priorities down to Five Passions they want to live for, as described in the next chapter.

My kids loved learning each other's priorities. As with the day a tornado threatened my kids, I didn't have to tell them what mattered most to them. They intuitively knew, but they hadn't thought it through. Therefore, they weren't yet ready to truly live it. They needed a forum like this to begin birthing a legacy that *they choose.* For example, Leslie sent me this note after completing the 50-20-5-1 Embrace exercise:

> I was blown away. People secretly want to narrow down their life philosophies and goals to see their hearts. They will be inspired to continue digging and convicted to re-evaluate what they are living for. The Holy Spirit is really released. People might think it's only them deciding and narrowing their lists, but certain ideas will come to mind that they would have never thought on their own. That happened to me, and I wasn't even asking for it.

Leslie wasn't the only one blown away. I was blown away by both her understanding and her newly-clarified vision. Paul Kimball wasn't expecting a new dream either, but his sacrificial priorities still blow me away. What about you? No matter where you are now, you can become a legacy maker like Paul. By helping your family funnel their pursuits into priorities, you'll help them transform successful living into sacrificial legacies.

Choices to practice:
1. Which priority primer is hardest for you – sacrifice, desperation, or dependence?

2. Who has selflessly sacrificed for you? What did they sacrifice?

3. Why aren't all pursuits worth sacrifice, desperation, and dependence?

Chapter 4

Five Passions

Six decades before my kids were born, the roots of their passions began. Rufus, a desperate Mexican laborer, traveled 1,900 miles with his wife and young kids to Wisconsin for a job. On the trip, though, Rufus became deathly ill. His wife, Soledad, faced the reality of being a foreign widow unable to speak English and no means of financial support. But she was also facing something else – a new kind of personal faith by some "strange" Americans who showered her with love. Still, she couldn't turn her back on tradition, at least not until she witnessed something in them that she couldn't explain away – their passion for compassion.

These strange Americans helped, expecting nothing in return. Their passion stirred a spiritual transformation in Soledad, which flowed into her son (my dad), then into me, and into my kids. Four generations and counting, all because anonymous born-again strangers poured their passion into others.

Undeniable passions impact unexpected people in unimaginable ways. This chapter helps you choose passions that can change eternity for someone, as well as their great grandkids, just like those selfless strangers did for Rufus and Soledad.

What propels passion in you? One of mine is leading my kids to choose well. But what young kid gets excited about choosing well? Not mine. So to connect with them, I combined something I'm good at – planning – with something I love to do – travel. Our vacations involved adventure, old churches, history, art, laughter, worship, food, sports, music, and more. I learned that indelible family memories can instill an indelible family faith.

On our "Alba men baseball trips," we did baseball games, mountain hiking, water rafting, museums, jazz clubs, ice cream, and much more, while talking about faith and family. They forgot the talks, but not the passion.

In Hawaii, we danced luaus, snorkeled coves, and hiked volcanos. But the highlight was attending church on a picturesque white-sand beach with a dozen native Hawaiians with a passionate faith, just like ours.

In Rome, I saw something grander than old churches and architecture. I saw something grand in my son. While gazing at the grandeur of St. Peter's Basilica and hearing about the sacrifices made to build it, Josh said, "Dad, it's too much. Why didn't they give all that money to feed the poor?" Wow. I saw Josh's passion for serving a majestic God, not a majestic building.

Vacations, like any passion, can align families with their treasures when they align both: 1) abilities – what you do well and 2) interests – what you love to do. Separately, abilities and interests are fun; together, they fulfill. Here's a little two-part exercise to help you realize your passions.

Part one begins by listing your abilities and interests, along with actions that could bring them together. For example, my passion for family vacations is the product of an ability to plan and an interest in travel.

Abilities	x	Interests	=	Passion
Planning		Travel		Vacations

Part two takes abilities and interests to another level. Beyond abilities (what you do well) is what God gives you to do. And beyond interests (what you love to do) is what God gives you to love. For when God is both the author and the audience, fun passions become fulfilling passions.

Our vacations were just fun trips until they instilled faith and family. Then they became tools to lead my kids to choose well. Our Alba men baseball trips became a receptivity-creating means of instilling faithfulness (and fun). Fulfilling passions are the product of multiplying what God gives you to do well and what God gives you to love.

God gives you to do well	x	God gives you to love	=	Fulfilling Passions
Planning		Travel		Vacations that lead kids to choose well

How well are you fulfilling your God-given gifts? On a scale of one to ten, you would need to be a ten in both to fulfill your potential (10 x 10, or 100%). If you're a seven in both, you might feel good about yourself, but you're missing over half of your opportunity (7 x 7, or only 49% fulfilled).

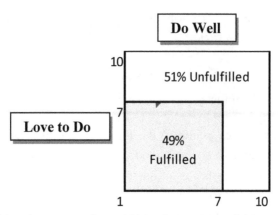

If either is a one, at least 90% of your potential is unfulfilled, even if the other is ten. Both must be significant in order to make a significant difference.

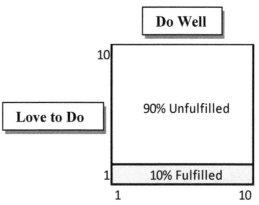

Doing something well without loving it will wear you out. The opposite – loving something but not doing it well – causes regret and disappointment. And lacking both is a recipe for disaster. God wants both – your abilities and interests, your hopes and dreams, your mind and heart. Therefore, we need to give Him the things for which we want to live – our Five Passions.

This is the hardest step yet of 50-20-5-1 because you're cutting priorities that matter most to you. These aren't necessarily five things you do now; they're five passions you *will* do . . . you *must* do. And since research shows that we can't focus on more than five to nine things, only a few can get your impassioned time, money and efforts.

Shifting to what can be

At this stage, 50-20-5-1 shifts. Picking pursuits and priorities is a vision of what you already treasure. Picking passions, however, is a vision of what you will treasure going forward – a shift from what is to what can be.

Five Passions go beyond priorities. Passions drive. Passions cut through the clutter (how you live) and get down to the bread and butter (why you live). They get you up, keep you going, and compel you to overcome. Passions draw from priorities but aren't limited to your actual past.

In writing your Five Passions in the 50-20-5-1, don't just circle five of your Twenty Priorities because passions are rarely described in just three words. Instead, elaborate and integrate the best parts of your priorities. Even if they don't yet describe you, ask God to give you five answers to: "I'm fulfilled when I …" and then write them in the 50-20-5-1 form at the end of Chapter 5 or the Workbook at www.timalba.com.

Considering the critical few causes you to reconsider the many. After choosing Five Passions, many people, including me, see the need to change their lists as well as their everyday priorities and pursuits. It highlights how "what is" often doesn't match with "what can be." In order to help you draw Five Passions from your Twenty Priorities, here's mine.

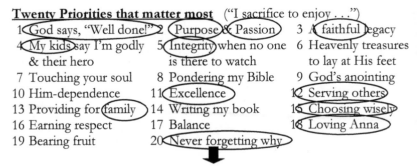

Twenty Priorities that matter most   ("I sacrifice to enjoy . . .")

1 God says, "Well done!" 2 Purpose & Passion   3 A faithful legacy
4 My kids say I'm godly   5 Integrity when no one   6 Heavenly treasures
& their hero   is there to watch   to lay at His feet
7 Touching your soul   8 Pondering my Bible   9 God's anointing
10 Him-dependence   11 Excellence   12 Serving others
13 Providing for family 14 Writing my book   15 Choosing wisely
16 Earning respect   17 Balance   18 Loving Anna
19 Bearing fruit   20 Never forgetting why

Five Passions I'll live for   ("I'm fulfilled when I . . .")

1 Hear God say, "Well done!"
2 Faithfully fulfill my God-given Purpose
3 Lead my family/others to choose wisely & never forget why
4 Love Anna (which flows to my kids)
5 Passionately pursue excellence with integrity

Predicting a family legacy – Session #2

In Session #2, everyone reads their Five Passions and shares why they want to live for those passions. It's a legacy predictor because your passions influence your kids' passions. Yes, exceptions occur, but kids who see godly legacies modeled well tend to follow well. If your passions compel you, your kids will likely want theirs to compel them too. Their passions will be unique, but they're often offshoots of yours. Based on your passions, what can you predict about your family's passions in years to come?

By aligning a family's (or work team's) passions, you can not only predict your future, you can also shape it. For example, before the 50-20-5-1 exercise existed, I led my work team to collaboratively choose their passions in a fun *Declaration of Interdependence*, which we signed every July 4th. Everyone received a signed, framed original declaration with a photo in a 1776 setting, with white wig, black robe, feather signing pen, and American flag. By sharing and aligning their passions, my team built community, improved results, and held each other accountable to *our* declared passions.

My family also created a declaration of our passions. I took my preteen and teenager kids to a special restaurant to open their imaginations, pitched the idea, and had them answer four questions: 1) What does our family stand for? 2) What songs symbolize our family? 3) What verses or phrases signify our family? and 4) What three to five words summarize our family?

I wrote a draft declaration using their answers, met with them again, and made changes to ensure it was *our* declaration, not mine. It taught me a key lesson – that kids really do pay attention, especially if we engage them in the process. For example, my thirteen-year-old son wanted our declaration to include, "when no one is watching." Why? Because he heard me often say that the true test of man is what he does in a hotel room when no one is watching. Wow. He had been listening after all, and he wanted it too. He just needed a forum to express it.

Before this exercise, my kids couldn't have explained what we stood for, but now they know. They just needed a forum to discover it. My family didn't need more truth; we needed truth to be made more real. The resulting *Declaration of Him-Dependence* (shown in chapter 6) didn't promise perfection, but it predicted who we would become.

Truth be told, my kids were initially a little underwhelmed with the idea of declaring passions. Just eye rolls and moans. So I made it fun, ending with photos and a signing ceremony in a 1776 setting, similar to my work declaration. As shown in Chapter 6, the signed declaration and goofy photos hang by our stairs as fun reminders. Our kids have forgotten the words, but they'll always remember their commitment to a family vision. And eight years later, our declaration led to an even more memorable tool that took our family vision to the next level: the 50-20-5-1 exercise.

While 50-20-5-1 doesn't involve photos or signing ceremonies, it also makes lasting impressions. Each family's experience is unique, but your family will surely cherish the memories you make doing 50-20-5-1 together. It prepared my kids to be like some of the greatest people I cherish but won't get to meet until heaven – those "strange" Americans who, by living out their passion for compassion nearly a century ago, changed eternity for four generations of Albas . . . and counting.

Choices to practice:

1. How have other people poured their passions into you?

2. Which priorities are hardest to cut to pick just Five Passions?

3. What passions hinder your faithfulness? What should replace them?

Note: Another great resource is *The Passion Test* by Janet Bray Attwood and Chris Attwood, which narrows ten or fifteen passions down to five inspirational passions. In 50-20-5-1, though, passions aren't the end; they're a motivating means to the next chapter – One Purpose.

Chapter 5

One Purpose

It was just another Saturday afternoon with my son. In fact, it was so long ago that he still thought I was cool. Anna phoned me in a panic, "A bad storm is coming. Drop everything and get home!" So I grabbed my young son and raced home to protect him (and my shiny red Miata convertible).

Amidst an ominous mid-day sky came the innocence of Caleb, barely able to peer over the dashboard when sitting on his knees, "Hey, Dad, look at the sun!" Confused, I replied, "What are you talking about, son?" So he pointed to a tiny distant ray of sunlight bursting through the dark clouds. All I had seen was danger. All Caleb saw was light. In reality, the light was already there. I just needed a little help to see it.

Years later, I bought a painting of a similar scene. Entitled *Peace in the Storm*, Phil Bob Borman paints golden rays of sunlight breaking through an ominous horizon, reminding me that peace is possible even if the darkest days. It's my visual reminder to "look at the Son" no matter what . . . to keep choosing my greatest treasures of faith and family.

We all like to visualize our treasures. Why else would we keep photos of family and friends? We don't need photos to love or remember them. But photos are strong visual reminders. Thus, if fleeing a burning home, Anna would grab photo albums that visualize her family's love – a purpose she will not live without.

What purpose won't you live without? Like me, you might not need a whole new purpose, just a little help seeing a purpose already there. This chapter helps you articulate that purpose, using purpose bifocals.

Purpose bifocals

My eyes were getting "foggy" as we got just twenty miles from our destination. After driving my son 1,800 miles to attend a music college in Boston with thousands of partying musicians, the reality of it all was sinking in. *Have I taught my son well? What will he do when I'm not around?* I knew my son's heart, but this would be a whole new test of his character and habits. I had held it together as we crossed through 11 states in two days, but as we neared Boston, I could no longer contain myself. My emotions burst forth, "Josh, all I ask of you is two things. If you'll do these two things, you'll make me proud and God proud. First, maximize your opportunity. And second, be faithful today."

In the many years since, I've realized that visionary purpose sees life through a similar lens – purpose bifocals – that seeks to: 1) maximize your opportunity and 2) be faithful today. Not one. Both. Dreams and actions. Possibilities and realities. Tomorrow's glory and today's faithfulness.

Living with purpose bifocals isn't easy, but it's not complicated. It enables you to surrender fully, sacrifice wholeheartedly, and submit fearlessly. You can filter out your clogging pursuits and funnel compelling purpose into others.

Funneling purpose is like compressing a flowing garden hose. Force builds by pressing your thumb on the end and holding it nearly shut. A trickle compresses into a projecting spray. Likewise, funneling your treasures turns dribbling pursuits into powerful streams of purpose.

The purpose you're funneling, though, must be yours, not someone else's. Copied treasures are not compelling treasures, at least not for long. Someone else's purpose can't satisfy you. Only you can lovingly live and unashamedly share your unique God-given purpose – the final step of 50-20-5-1. You'll narrow five passions that you'll live for down to one purpose you won't live without – your "One Purpose." This isn't a purpose you prefer, manufacture, or aspire to; it's a purpose God gives you (2 Timothy 1:9). It oozes from your pores. In order to articulate it, consider the examples of Simon Peter and David.

Simon Peter was a rock upon which Jesus would build His church (Matthew 16:18). An uneducated fisherman turned the world upside down when his purpose aligned with Jesus' purpose. Just imagine what you could do if your purpose aligned with His.

David was a man after God's own heart (1 Samuel 13:14). David didn't wait for prominence, though, to be purposeful. His heart emulated God's heart, which enabled him to slay Goliath and later become king. So too, who knows how God could use your purpose if it aligns with His.

I'm not trying to tell you what your purpose is. Books like Rick Warren's *The Purpose Driven Life* can help with that. I'm challenging you to ensure that your purpose leads to God's embrace. But you have to know it first. And to truly know it, you have to succinctly state it. It's like one of the many incredible communication lessons taught by Dianna Booher: "If you can't write your message in a sentence, you can't say it in an hour."

As God refined me, I kept refining my stated purpose until it told my story in one sentence. Then again, God often takes us through seasons of refining simplification because they not only drive us to our purpose, they also drive us to our knees.

Your One Purpose should be a declaration of who you can be, even if you're not yet that person. It's not a new year's resolution; it's a new life resolve of who you want to be when standing before a holy God. It's your answer to: "I feel God's embrace when I . . ."

In crafting your One Purpose, don't just pick one of your passions. Find the parts of your Five Passions that you can't live without and write them in one sentence that reflects your heart and compels your soul. To help you write your One Purpose, here's how mine flows from my Five Passions.

Five Passions I'll live for   ("I'm fulfilled when I am . . .")
1 Hearing God say, "Well done!"
2 Being faithful to fulfill my God-given Purpose
3 Leading my family/others to choose wisely & never forget why
4 Loving Anna (which flows to my kids)
5 Passionately pursuing excellence with integrity

One Purpose I won't live without   ("I feel God's embrace when I . . .")
To help my family and others want what they need to be faithful

"Well done!"

My One Purpose captivates my soul and tells my story – a story of a simple man pursuing what truly matters, a story of a husband and dad trying to lead and connect with loved ones, a story of a learner striving to be faithful in good times and bad. It may or may not inspire you, but it convicts and compels me. It's not a fancy story, but it's mine, and I must live it, just as you must live yours, in order to feel God's embrace.

In *The Power of Vision*, George Barna says that grasping this for you is "exciting to behold. Indeed, embracing and carrying out that vision will bring you unimaginable gratification and fulfillment." Your One Purpose is your declaration to God of what He wants to declare through you . . . your gift to back to God and others based on all God has so graciously given you.

For many years, my stated purpose was "to faithfully fulfill my God-given purpose." Yes, that's vague, but it's how I see purpose – it's in everything. Purpose consumes me, maybe too much at times, because it changes everything. For example, I told my little kids that my parenting purpose was to raise holy kids, not happy kids. Why? I wanted them to be happy, but happiness wasn't my goal. Happiness flows from holiness, not vice versa. That's why we created a *Declaration of **Him**-dependence*, not a *Declaration of **Happiness**-dependence*.

I had to learn, though, that purpose must be specific, personal, and practical. I still want to faithfully fulfill my God-given purpose, but I needed to clarify how.

What parts of your Five Passions could clarify a purpose you can't imagine living without? In writing your One Purpose in the 50-20-5-1 form at the end of this chapter, please remember that if it doesn't maximize your opportunity and cause you to be faithful, keep reworking it.

Declaring your purpose doesn't control kids; it directs the heritage they inherit. For example, the key to Anna's purpose is that she pours it into our kids. God does the pouring; she holds the funnel. Our kids didn't understand it at first, but they did over time as she kept pouring. What is flowing out of your family's funnel and how is it directing your kids?

Directing a family legacy – Session #2 continues

Directing legacies is all about positioning. A boxing champion was asked why his opponents' heads were always in the same position before he knocked them out. The champ replied, "Because I hit it there." Granted, we'd never hit kids into place, but we can help position them into a place of receptivity.

In the finale of Session #2, everyone reads aloud their One Purpose and shares why it's so important to them. Also, discuss the similarities of your family members' 50-20-5-1 visions and unpack each person's uniquenesses. Josh wrote concise, practical lists, while Caleb's sharp insights were like a samurai cutting through clutter. Leslie struggled to narrow her many deep thoughts. Despite their dissimilarities, however, I saw a family resemblance. Each child's purpose was like a piece of a common family pie, yet with its own unique flavor. For example, my musician son, Josh, calls his purpose: "Being in tune with God."

50-20-5-1 also impacts kids in ways you'd never expect. I was surprised to read this from Caleb, my previously non-communicative teenage son:

> I want to use this list with my future family and annually with myself to see how I've grown. We should do this again later because it allowed us to grow closer to one another. I'll definitely edit my list and make it applicable. It's a great process but, if not backed up with action, it's just a list. It's useful if refined over years of growth and change. But it shouldn't stop there. The list should be composed of goals that propel me to action.

I was even more surprised at what happened five years later at Christmas – my kids gave me updated 50-20-5-1 visions. I saw how their pursuits and priorities had changed as their life stages changed, and how their passions and purposes were similar, yet refined as they had matured. Even better, they were beginning to shape their own family visions.

You might update your 50-20-5-1 visions on anniversaries, birthdays, or Christmas. Or you might put updated lists in a picture frame for each person, like annual school portraits. Regardless of the method used, expect to see the miracle of your family's purpose come alive.

The miracle of purpose

If you saw the February 1980 Olympics, you likely recall Al Michaels saying, "Do you believe in miracles? Yes!" It was David versus Goliath, and David won. A whole country celebrated when the USA hockey team upset the mighty Soviets. Players hugged, shouted with joy, and skated victory laps.

In February 1980, I lived my own sports miracle. Although my high school basketball team won only three of sixteen games, we made the playoffs (actually, every team made the playoffs in Iowa). We were bad. Really bad. Still, we somehow won two playoff games. Up next, though, was a tall, talented rival that had embarrassed us a few weeks earlier. We had no chance. How could we even compete against these Goliaths? Our only hope was a secret weapon we unleashed that night.

What was that secret weapon? It was our lucky shoes, of course, which we spray painted orange! Goofy plan? Sure, but it worked. We won and celebrated like we'd beaten the Soviets. We cut down the nets, hugged, shouted with joy, and drove victory laps on my little town's main street.

Granted, our victory didn't compare to the USA hockey team, but both helped me believe in miracles. And other than our lucky orange shoes, both occurred because of the miracle of purpose. Eric Liddell, though, didn't need lucky shoes to have legendary purpose.

Liddell was favored to win gold in the 1924 Olympics, but he wouldn't run his race because it occurred on Sunday. Instead of violating his convictions, he ran another race and miraculously won. The reason Liddell wouldn't sacrifice personal glory for personal convictions was captured in the movie *Chariots of Fire*: "I believe that God made me for a purpose. But He also made me fast. And when I run, I feel His pleasure." Running was a tool to fulfill his purpose of proclaiming Jesus Christ.

Pursuing your purpose can become a pleasure too, even if it's not the race you prefer. Ask yourself: In whatever God made me to do, do I feel His pleasure in doing it? If you're a coach, you can say: I believe God made me for a purpose, but He also made me to coach. When my players perform, I feel His pleasure.

If you're a teacher . . . I believe God made me for a purpose, but He also made me to teach. When my students learn, I feel His pleasure.

If you're a parent . . . I believe God made me for a purpose, but He also made me a parent. When my kids mature, I feel His pleasure."

When players perform, students learn, and kids mature, others are blessed. Feeling God's pleasure is great, but pleasure is selfish if not multiplied through others. Liddell saw this purpose first in his father, who said in *Chariots of Fire*: "You can praise God by peeling a spud if you peel it to perfection . . . Run in God's name and let the world stand back in wonder."

Liddell's father helped him enjoy victory laps on the track by preparing him for victory laps in heaven. And so can you. Imagine being in heaven, cheering your family to complete what you started. With arms outstretched, they'll cross their finish line and embrace you. Reunited. Jubilant. Savoring their long-awaited victory lap with all those who helped them win.

How are you preparing for heavenly victory laps? With whom do you want to celebrate? Even if it will take a miracle for them to join you in heaven, how could you help them? Whatever it may be, it's your gift to *God* that benefits *them* and fulfills *you* . . . in that order. It's how your purpose becomes the miracle they need, even if they don't yet realize it.

Having your family join you in heavenly victory laps depends largely on the beliefs you model and the bonds you make. For example, Max Lucado writes incredible books, but I admire him more for his incredible daughter, Sara. As Leslie's college roommate, Sara's life validated how godly families share elements of a common purpose. Sara's dad was famous; Leslie's dad, not. But both girls did what they were prepared to do – run their race in order to receive their Heavenly Father's embrace.

Fame isn't important to God; child-like faith is – faith like little Ryan Christian. A young cancer fighter, Ryan Christian's infectious smile and joy would make any parent proud. While praying for a miracle, she never lost sight of what mattered most, reportedly saying, "When I get to heaven, I want God to know who I am." Imagine little Ryan's heavenly victory lap as she crossed her finish line and hugged the God who knew her so well.

With child-like faith like Ryan, we can believe in miracles and see a light already there. And with their parents' help, kids can see another miracle . . . the miracle of becoming who they were created to be, while also being grateful for who they are. My kids became receptive largely because they saw their mom joyfully becoming who she was created to be. Anna doesn't talk about running a race, pursuing a purpose, or positioning a life funnel. She's connects with our kids by being purely relational. Here's how she summarized the 50-20-5-1 Embrace exercise from her loving mom's perspective:

> How sweet to hear our kids' hopes and dreams. It was humbling and a blessing. Much of their lists aligned with the legacy we passed down, but some went further. I look forward to seeing them grow and their lists evolve. I loved thinking through my own list and seeing on paper what I've known in my heart to be my purpose. What a great family experience.

Take the challenge. Cast the vision. Complete 50-20-5-1 with your family. Then strap on for a blessing that can change your family's legacy. The next chapter gives six practical examples of how to turn individual family member's treasures into a powerful family vision that each family member can embrace as their own.

Choices to practice:

1. How could you maximize your purpose and bless your kids?

2. How could you position your family to be faithful?

3. What purpose causes you to feel God's pleasure?

Before moving to practical applications of family vision, if you hadn't done so already, please take a moment to complete your 50-20-5-1 vision below. As Henriette Anne Klauser says in *Write It Down and Make It Happen,* put your heart on paper, write your most extravagant wishes, actively realize them, frequently review them, and share them with someone who loves you enough to hold you accountable to follow through.

50-20-5-1-Embrace

Fifty Pursuits that matter   ("I'm happy when enjoying. . .")

1 _____	2 _____	3 _____
4 _____	5 _____	6 _____
7 _____	8 _____	9 _____
10 _____	11 _____	12 _____
13 _____	14 _____	15 _____
16 _____	17 _____	18 _____
19 _____	20 _____	21 _____
22 _____	23 _____	24 _____
25 _____	26 _____	27 _____
28 _____	29 _____	30 _____
31 _____	32 _____	33 _____
34 _____	35 _____	36 _____
37 _____	38 _____	39 _____
40 _____	41 _____	42 _____
43 _____	44 _____	45 _____
46 _____	47 _____	48 _____
49 _____	50 _____	

⬇

Twenty Priorities that matter most   ("I sacrifice to enjoy . . .")

1 _____	2 _____	3 _____
4 _____	5 _____	6 _____
7 _____	8 _____	9 _____
10 _____	11 _____	12 _____
13 _____	14 _____	15 _____
16 _____	17 _____	18 _____
19 _____	20 _____	

⬇

Five Passions I'll live for   ("I'm fulfilled when I am . . .")

1 _____
2 _____
3 _____
4 _____
5 _____

⬇

One Purpose I won't live without   ("I feel God's embrace when I . . .")
My One Purpose   _____

⬇

"Well done!"

55

Examples of Pursuits
(to personalize for your Fifty Pursuits)

Family	Career	Chocolate	Beautiful sunsets
Kids/Grandkids	Marriage	Music	Bubble baths
Heaven	Rebuking lies	Quiet	Good hair days
Faith	Intimacy	Happiness	Friends that get me
Financial security	Safety	Fun	Cold drink/hot day
Clear conscious	Beauty	Growth	Flowers
Hope	"I love you"	"Thank you"	"I'm sorry"
Achieving goals	Imagination	Sales	Mentoring
Vacation	Graduation	Going home	Homemade gifts
Independence	Hugs	New baby	Broadway shows
Heating & A/C	Awards	Legacy	Good coffee
Encouragement	Pets	Hobbies	Second chances
Family reunions	Humility	Confidence	Being appreciated
God's presence	Salvation	Peace	Accountable friends
Acceptance	Forgiveness	Gentleness	Unconditional love
Eyesight	Balance	Belly laugh	Creativity
Addiction free	Bible/Church	Pain free	Military service
Patriotism	Freedom	Protection	Counting blessings
Good judgment	Courage	Quality time	Fresh perspective
Memories	Planning	Fellowship	The perfect outfit
Bearing fruit	Birthdays	Anniversaries	Laugh at yourself
Leadership	Patience	Great car	Joy in the journey
Wise choices	Marital sex	Mobility	Using your gifts
Fulfillment	Faithfulness	Missions	Ability to choose
Favorite schools	Transparency	Work ethic	One-on-one talks
Transformation	Christmas	Identity	Make others proud
Excellence	Adventures	Competition	Rebuking lies
Vulnerability	Role models	Sports teams	Acts of kindness
Physical fitness	Respect	Snow	Being barefoot
Compassion	Trust	Naps	Cheap airfares
Adoption	Education	Retirement	Saving babies
Home cooking	Being crazy	Restful sleep	Medical healing

Tim's 50-20-5-1 Embrace

Fifty Pursuits that matter ("I'm happy when enjoying. . .")

1. God says, "Well done!" 2. Purpose & Passion 3. A faithful legacy
4. My kids say I'm godly & their hero 5. Integrity when no one is there to watch 6. Heavenly treasures to lay at His feet
7. Anna's embrace 8. Loving Anna 9. Compelling "whys"
10. God's anointing 11. Content, not satisfied 12. Serving others
13. Providing for family 14. Mom's enchiladas 15. Choosing wisely
16. "Nuggets" of hope 17. Earning respect 18. Writing my book
19. Touching your soul 20. Good judgment 21. Persistence
22. Making Dad proud 23. True friendship 24. Excellence
25. Surrendering to God 26. Using unique gifts 27. "Shameless" praise
28. Answered prayers 29. Purposeful paintings 30. Family's laughter
31. Pondering my Bible 32. Balance 33. Great music (loud)
34. Proactively change 35. Hot showers 36. Exploring/traveling
37. Tenacious work ethic 38. Historical churches 39. CiCi's Pizza
40. Executing plans 41. Hawkeye football 42. Him-dependence
43. Bearing fruit 44. Health & Exercise 45. Always learning
46. Defending freedom 47. Solving problems 48. Real leadership
49. Never forgetting why 50. Finishing strong

Twenty Priorities that matter most ("I sacrifice to enjoy . . .")

1. God says, "Well done!" 2. Purpose & Passion 3. A faithful legacy
4. My kids say I'm godly & their hero 5. Integrity when no one is there to watch 6. Heavenly treasures to lay at His feet
7. Touching your soul 8. Pondering my Bible 9. God's anointing
10. Him-dependence 11. Excellence 12. Serving others
13. Providing for family 14. Writing my book 15. Choosing wisely
16. Earning respect 17. Balance 18. Loving Anna
19. Bearing fruit 20. Never forgetting why

Five Passions I'll live for ("I'm fulfilled when I am . . .")

1. Hearing God say, "Well done!"
2. Being faithful to fulfill my God-given Purpose
3. Leading my family/others to choose wisely & never forget why
4. Loving Anna (which flows to my kids)
5. Passionately pursuing excellence with integrity

One Purpose I won't live without ("I feel God's embrace when I . . .")
To help my family and others want what they need to be faithful

"Well done!"

Chapter 6

Vision Monuments

"Hmmm. Maybe that would fit Josh. If only it was that easy . . ."

Protective parental instincts were kicking in as Josh and I stared blankly at medieval armor at the Met in New York City. Instead of enjoying art, we were utterly exhausted from moving him into a rundown one-room apartment in Harlem. It was so sketchy that Josh had to unlock four sets of doors to get from the lobby to his room. It didn't help when he said, "Don't worry, I carry a knife." That's not what you want to hear from a young, diminutive son moving 1,600 miles from home.

Despite no job or local friends, Josh had picked that meager, dangerous apartment to pursue his dreams. I'll never forget his pale, helpless face as I waved goodbye and rode away in a yellow taxi. It broke my heart. What would happen when I couldn't be there to protect him? Had I prepared him for his new life? Should I have let him move there? If only I could have covered him somehow with that armor, I would have felt much better.

Centuries ago, armor offered protection, but now it's hard to find the right size at Armors-R-Us. If only it was that easy. Since we can't use armor, kids need something that only parents can provide – something that protects them when we're not around and prepares them when they're out on their own.

We wish we could control our kids' paths, but we can't. We instruct. We correct. We pray. But we protect and prepare them to walk their own path by experiencing a home culture of vivid faithfulness and visual reminders of the fruit of faithfulness. Then, even if you're tearfully dropping off your son in Harlem, he's ready for whatever happens next. And, hey, if that doesn't work, he has a knife, right?!

While 50-20-5-1 is a framework to choose your treasures, this chapter makes your treasures come alive using "vision monuments" – visual symbols of your life treasures. Cities like Washington D.C were built around symbolic monuments of valued people and memories. Families can do the same. Not with statues, but with symbolic monuments in our homes that visually tell our life stories and create a vivid culture of values.

Vision monuments turn family vision into powerful living, like a family version of Simon Sinek description of leadership in *Start With Why*: "a vision of the world that does not yet exist and the ability to communicate it." Does your home communicate the family values to which you aspire, even if those values don't yet fully exist? This chapter shows you how to start. For even when your kids act like they don't care, they do. My kids didn't seem to care either, but years later I overheard them telling friends the stories behind our home decor.

Vision monuments help you parent for the long term by putting family treasures in action and teaching why. For indeed, godly treasures are both caught and taught. Kids need to see godly treasures lived out in practical ways and need to understand why they matter so much. Vision monuments do that by helping kids see who your family is and who you want to become. Here are six examples to help you visualize your own family vision.

Love monuments

People may know you love them, but they cherish knowing why. Photos, signs, heirlooms, and much more can be love monuments – visual ways of expressing love. The best ones speak their language. A great place to start is Gary Chapman's *The Five Love Languages*: gifts, quality time, words of affirmation, acts of service, and physical touch.

My wife's love language is words of affirmation. So on her 50th birthday, I gave her a list. Nothing screams romance like a list, right? Well, it can when it speaks her language. This list, called *Fifty Reasons It's a Privilege to be Your Husband*, connected with her because behind each "reason" is a story of love. Anna cried, told her friends, and posted it on our refrigerator for years.

Fifty Reasons It's a Privilege to be Your Husband

1. Leslie, Joshua & Caleb
2. Your heart still skips a beat
3. My best friend
4. Salado
5. Always believing in me
6. Gracious spirit
7. Unquestioned loyalty
8. Deep spiritual roots
9. Choosing the library
10. Hugs
11. Smiles
12. Fun
13. Back scratches
14. "Is this the Trevi Fountain?"
15. Molokai mule rides
16. Caring for our parents
17. Master of the simple recipe
18. Skiing your way – slowww
19. Forgiving quickly
20. Seeing the good in others
21. Praising God
22. Choosing to love me
23. Laughing at my jokes
24. Being a "china doll"
25. Completing me
26. Love me more than chocolate
27. Passing on "Family Recipes"
28. Understanding my passion
29. Celebrating little victories
30. Saying, "Enough" as needed
31. Living a godly legacy
32. Respecting me no matter what
33. Refusing to fight
34. Our Home Field Advantage
35. Living in the moment
36. True hospitality
37. Loving other people's children
38. Venturing with Vacation Tim
39. Watching guy movies with me
40. Finding the positive
41. Praying for our family
42. Trusting my judgment
43 "Good thing I'm cute"
44. "Gotta love me"
45. Making me smell the roses
46. Helping me pursue my dreams
47. Hurting with others who hurt
48. Being consistently kind
49. 28 incredible years + 3
50. Living "Well done!"

I knew that Anna loved her list, but I had no idea my kids did too. A year later, what did I get on Father's Day? A tie? Gift card? No. My kids surprised me with their own list: *Fifty Reasons You Are an Awesome Father.* It was like a greatest hits album of family memories. Some of their fifty reasons were unique to one child; others were shared by all. Some were big events; others, everyday priorities. It reinforced how much kids love to see Dad love his wife and how much kids need a forum to express their own love.

Still, in the dog days, parents question themselves. Me too. But my kids' list – their own love monument – gave me answers, some of which I'll share in this chapter. Another answer came from my daughter-in-law, Robyn, who told Anna, "I love how Tim loves you. It gives me hope that Josh will keep loving me the same way when we're your age." Beyond a sweet way of saying we're old, Robyn was catching our family culture.

Love monuments touch the soul, even if you don't understand why. I don't know why Anna loves her rarely-used China cabinet or a painting of elegant moms and daughters sipping tea. Anna knows I don't care about China cabinets and tea sippers, but she loves them even more because they visualize my love for her and the kids who were watching.

How could you express love that speaks your family's language? The possibilities are as endless as your imagination.

Heritage monuments

Heritage monuments don't create a heritage; they visualize it. For example, man-caves and offices often have trophies with back stories. In Chris Burton's office hangs a behemoth stuffed turkey, not because it's a hobby, but because it's a heritage his dad used to engage Chris and his kids. That's when godly heritages get passed down – when kids buy in – like when we created our family Declaration of Him-dependence, as mentioned in Chapter 4.

Declaration of Him-Dependence

We, the Alba family, declare our absolute, utter dependence
upon You – the Lord Jesus Christ.

We choose to serve you – and You alone.
We worship You – because You are worthy.
We confess it's not about us – You deserve all the glory.
We testify our love to You – by sharing and caring for others.
We passionately pursue Your purpose – when no one is watching.
We remember the price You paid and gift you gave – to save us.
We surrender our hopes & dreams to You – and know we are safe.
We kneel before You–and You raise us up to more than we can be.
We lay up our treasures – to hear You say,
"Well done, good and faithful servants!"
We lay our crowns at Your feet – and feel Your embrace forever.
We can hardly wait for the day we're Safely Home – with you.

Kids need visionary statements, but they especially need visionary parents. Our declaration was a great experience, but I still wondered if it really mattered to my kids. My answer came a decade later in reason #18 of my kids' *Fifty Reasons You Are an Awesome Father* list: "Leading your family in writing the *Declaration of Him-dependence*." And in Chapter 12, you'll read my son's letter that referenced what this declaration means to him.

What family heritages are you passing down and how could you visualize them?

Faith Monuments

Faith monuments visualize faith, connect believers, and honor eternity-minded heroes. Remember Grandpa Loyd's Bible in Chapter 1 that reflected his devoted, well-worn life? Another example is a painting by Kathy Fincher of three kids doing sign language of "Jesus loves me." It symbolizes how Anna taught our kids to love a Savior who loved them first.

My faith monuments don't force faith. They're tools to fulfill my One Purpose from Chapter 5: "to help my family and others want what they need to be faithful." They're conduits for others to want their own abiding faith.

Faith monuments are also conversation starters. For example, a fabric of African warriors hangs in my office. My daughter brought it back from a Uganda mission trip and said, "Dad, when I saw those warriors, I thought of you." It's one of my favorite gifts because it visualizes how she chooses to see her daddy's faith, not his faults. The cost to buy this fabric was paltry, but the emotions it stirs are priceless.

How could you visualize your faith? What's already in your home that you hadn't thought of as being a faith monument?

Passion Monuments

What lights your fire and keeps it burning? Whatever it is, visualize it. Passion monuments show why you're decidedly focused, deeply personal, and desperately real. They inspire kids to consider their own passions.

A great place to start is your Five Passions in Chapter 4. Since one of mine is "passionately pursue excellence with integrity," Anna had a sketch drawn of two hands reaching for a trapeze bar, along with a favorite quote: "Throw your heart across the bar and the rest will follow." It reflects the focus, conviction, and practice that excellence requires.

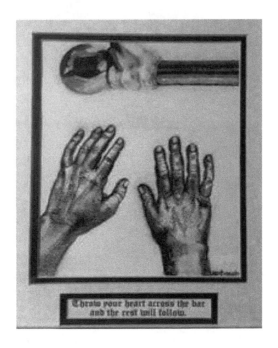

How could your home inspire your kids' passions?

Financial Monuments

Financial monuments show the real value of money. My dad taught me that people find a way to afford what they value. He's right. Our trophies reflect our treasures. My dad lives with a generous spirit, so he sees money as a tool for blessing others. My favorite financial monument isn't a trophy of my career successes; rather, it's a cheap three-inch wood carving from my dad.

Why a Hawaiian "hang loose" souvenir? Because of the story it tells. In order to give my kids a biblical view of money, I led them in a Crown Financial Ministries Bible study. Yes, they were underwhelmed! No kid shouts, "Party!" for a financial Bible study, right? Well, they did when it was tied to a Hawaii trip to bless their grandparents. That little hang loose carving silently shouts lessons learned on tithing, saving, and generosity.

Based on my kids' spending habits, though, I wondered if those lessons had stuck. A decade later, the answer came – reason #17 of their *Fifty Reasons* Fathers' Day list: "Leading your family in a financial Bible study." They've forgotten many of the details, but they remember that money will draw you either closer to God or away from Him . . . a choice only they can make.

How could money draw you closer to God and family?

Memories Monuments

While faith and family are the cornerstones of well-done legacies, we need glue to fill in the cracks. As we'll see in Chapter 14, the glue that bonds faith and family is cherished memories. But does your home reflect the memories you want your kids to cherish?

Rather than filling your home with "stuff," fill it with visual reminders of your greatest memories. Everything in our home has a story, and our kids know those stories because we tell them. For example, my kids joke about all my paintings, even though they know why these paintings mean so much to me – they're visual reminders of our family's values and of memories created while spending time together in distant lands or just down the road.

Still, we all wonder sometimes if anything is working because kids rarely, if ever, tell us, right? Well, take heart. I didn't know either until I saw reason #47 of my kids' *Fifty Reasons* Father's Day list: "Letting your art reflect the way you truly live your life."

But what do you do when kids don't respond? When you're worn out from potty training, training wheels, training bras, or drivers training? The answer is: look for your version of Mavericks tickets.

Your Mavericks Tickets

Unlike his extroverted siblings, the best you'd get from teenager Caleb was an occasional grunt or nod. Therefore, I tried the one thing I knew he liked – Dallas Mavericks basketball. Dreams of dad-and-son bonding danced in my mind as I bought a ten-game package of Mavericks tickets.

What happened? He loved it . . . for four games. Then he lost interest and stopped going. Seriously?! I rearranged my hectic life to spend quality time with a son whose love language is quality time. And he didn't care! Five years later, however, I was shocked by reason #46 of my kids' *Fifty Reasons* Father's Day list: "Mavericks season tickets."

Turns out, Caleb actually did care. So why did a non-responsive teenager secretly cherish basketball games he didn't attend? Because he knew I wanted to spend quality time together. He was secretly catching our family vision.

If you too ever struggle with non-responsive kids, be encouraged. Don't let your kids' responses determine your preparation. No matter how they respond, keep trusting. Keep investing. Keep casting vision. You never know what will be your version of Mavericks tickets – secretly cherished memories.

I ask our parenting seminar attendees to look around their homes for vision monuments. For example, in our entryway is *Safely Home*, an inspiring painting by Ron DiCianni. We didn't call it a monument or vision armor, but it symbolized a family vision that protected and prepared my kids, whether they were safely home or in a dangerous place with nothing but a knife.

Just remember . . . we demonstrate; they emulate. We don't tell kids exactly what to do or how to feel. We give visionary direction, not a GPS program with turn-by-turn directions.

Vision monuments creatively provide a compass and a map. They point kids in the right direction, show them how to get there, and stir them to want to get there in their own unique ways.

What vision monuments are in your home? You surely have them, even if you don't yet realize it. What stories do they tell? Do they capture your kids' imagination? Do they create a culture that helps kids want what they need to be faithful? Kids don't need anything fancy, just visual reminders of what you treasure and, as we'll see next, the timeless character to back it up.

Choices to practice:

1. What kind of vision do you want your family to embrace?

2. How could you visualize your love?

3. What cherished memories did you secretly treasure as a kid?

CHARACTER

(TREASURE YOUR CHOICES)

"But store up for yourselves treasures in heaven, where neither moth nor rust destroys, and where thieves do not break in or steal; for where your treasure is, there your heart will be also" (Matthew 6:20-21).

"The righteous man who walks in his integrity – how blessed are his sons after him" (Proverbs 20:7).

Chapter 7

1-2-3-U Discovery

"I'm desperate!" In tears, my co-worker Lori pleaded, "Tim, you *have* to pray for my sister! She has cancer with only weeks to live. I'm so scared. We need a miracle. It's our only hope!"

So we prayed fervently. We trusted desperately. And a few weeks later, we praised unashamedly when Lori stopped me with a tearful glow and proclaimed, "Tim, guess what. My sister's cancer is gone ... completely! The doctors can't explain it, but we know why. It's God! It's totally God! He's so amazing! Thank you so much for praying. Can you believe it?!"

Two tearful conversations with two exponentially different emotions. Lori's sister didn't deserve terminal cancer nor did she earn miraculous healing. Amidst both utter awe and utter desperation, Lori held to one constant – the character to trust. Therefore, I sent Lori these thirteen words, which God has used to sustain me through my own trials over the years:

Sometimes we stand in awe.
Sometimes we kneel in desperation.
Always we trust.

We can't control life, but we can choose how to walk it. No matter the pain, we can trust. Death knocks, cancer returns, money disappears, kids wander, spouses quit, or friends betray. What sustains us then? It isn't the time-tested confidence gained from working harder. It's the timeless character honed from trusting fuller, whether times are really good or really bad.

Timeless character is within us all. Yes, it's revealed in trials, but it's also received from God who freely offers it. The more we receive God's character, the more we trust it and the more it flows through us and into our kids.

Timeless character – living your chosen qualities with integrity – is real and relational. It's trustworthy and transparent. Ageless and authentic. Parents with timeless character don't perform for God; they reform for Him. When they don't live up to their desired quality characteristics (no one does), the quality of their character shines through in their response. And when their actual path isn't their preferred path, they find the grit to keep putting their kids on the path to faithfulness.

In *Wooden on Leadership*, John Wooden says: "Before you can lead others, you must be able to lead yourself." Nowhere is this truer than in families. Leading kids well starts with leading yourself well. As Scotty Sanders often asks: "Would you follow you?" How well are you leading you . . . really? Here's a quick reality challenge to help you begin answering that question.

A Reality Challenge

It's universal. Four billion men share one fear. They want to avoid death, taxes, starvation, financial ruin, and loneliness, but the one thing every man fears is "the look" from his wife, mother, or grandmother. My wife gives me the look even when I haven't said a word. I'm proud of what I don't say, yet I'm in trouble for what I'm thinking! How's that fair?! Fair or not, I might as well apologize because we both know she's right. But how can Anna peg me, yet not understand her own feelings? It's because she knows my character – the real me. I need her candor to enlighten the blind spots I can't see and often don't know exist. Here are three questions as a preview for discovering the reality of who you really are – your true character.

Reality challenge #1: How do you spend your time?

Look at your calendar, planner, sticky notes, or time organizer. Where does your time really go? It goes to whatever you treasure most at that moment, even if you think something else matters more. For example, you may want faith or family to be #1, but does your time tell a different story? Whatever gets your best time is, in reality, your greatest treasure.

Next is reality challenge #2: How do you use your money?

Whether you're a saver or spender, your budget, bank statement, or credit card bills are proof of what you treasure. Money goes wherever your heart is, in relationships, in work, and in everything. Time and money are never neutral. They're magnets. Depending on how you hold onto them, time and money are either pulling you closer to God or away from Him. In which direction are money and time pulling you?

Last, here's reality challenge #3: What gets your best efforts?

How can I say I love Anna and God, but not give them my best? Anna is gracious, yet she expects my best, which I promised her on March 17, 1984. A gracious God also expects my best, which I promised Him when I surrendered my life to Him. Neither requires perfection; just my best.

In the parable of the talents in Matthew 25, a master gives five talents, two talents, and one talent to three servants. The servant with five talents gives his best efforts, doubles his master's investment, and is rewarded with five more. The servant with two talents doubles his too and gets two more. The third servant, who buries his one talent, is unprepared and unexpectant for his master's return, and is eternally punished.

What the master loves and rewards is faithfulness. He doesn't require the same results, but he won't tolerate not trying. The third servant's intentions may be good, but his character isn't. He doesn't blow his talent; he blows his opportunity.

What the two faithful servants fear is something scarier than their wives' "look." They fear the master's look of disappointment. And they can't wait to see the proud look on his face. Yes, we enter heaven's door through faith in Jesus, but heaven's welcome mat is sown with the reality of our character.

Kids with timeless character are birthed from parents with timeless character. These parents give their best because nothing less will do. They honor God by redeeming time, leveraging money, and giving best efforts. Even if it's not what they prefer; it's what God expects and kids need. Sometimes, though, it takes the horror of near tragedy to discover the character to live for our treasures. It did for me one day . . .

It would have been just another work day, except for the anticipation of seeing my newborn son, Caleb. I pulled into the driveway clueless that everything was about to change.

I walked in, saw their terrified faces, and knew something was horribly wrong. Anna had called 9-1-1 because my precious newborn was blue and lifeless, slumped over in his infant swing. As Anna was about to begin infant CPR, little Caleb gasped and miraculously started breathing again.

We never learned why Caleb nearly died, so we never knew if, or when, piercing ambulance sirens would again come for him. For months, I lived with the fear of a dying child, as Caleb's monitor blared whenever his chest stopped moving for a few seconds. Many nights we were jolted awake by the alarm of a near-lifeless baby who soon resumed breathing. I never knew if this time would be the last time I hugged my son.

I didn't need a hypothetical question of what I'd grab amidst crisis. I was living it. In those moments of truth, you discover the real you – if what you *say* matters actually *does*. But as dark days of fear turned into years of everyday living, I learned that blaring monitors drive us to your knees, but they don't keep us there. We need something to sustain our focus whether life is good or bad. It's the flip side of choosing your treasures . . . treasuring your choices.

Take a quarter and look at George Washington. Now turn it over. What do you see? It depends on how you flip it. If, like most people, you turn a coin from side to side like shuffling pages, it's not what you expected. You have to turn it upside down for it to make sense. That's how treasuring your choices works too. You have to turn things upside down. Well-done parents don't shuffle. They turn today's drama into tomorrow's dreams. For as important as it is to have a compelling family vision, what difference does it make without the character to back it up?

Vision without character is untrusted, and character without vision is aimless. Visionary character, though, draws kids to want the virtuous qualities they're beginning to understand. The second bond of well-done parenting – treasuring your choices – reveals that timeless character within us all. And the 1-2-3-U Discovery is an assessment to help you make timeless character your reality and put your kids on the path to faithfulness.

1-2-3-U Discovery

The 1-2-3-U Discovery helps you lead yourself well so that you can lead your family well. It builds a culture of character that kids respect and emulate. While 50-20-5-1 clarifies *vision* to choose your treasures, 1-2-3-U flips it over with *character* to treasure those choices. 50-20-5-1 distills passions and purpose; whereas, 1-2-3-U turns purpose-fulfilling passion into success, success into significance, and significance into faithfulness.

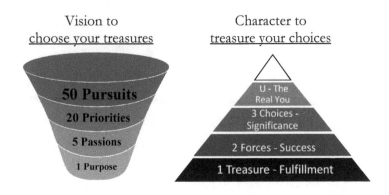

Vision to
choose your treasures

Character to
treasure your choices

50 Pursuits

20 Priorities

5 Passions

1 Purpose

U - The
Real You

3 Choices -
Significance

2 Forces - Success

1 Treasure - Fulfillment

You can't force timeless character into your kids, but you can help them mold it and discover it regardless of the circumstances. As Dr. Jim Dennison noted in his inspiring daily blog, *The Daily Article*: "Nothing about our circumstances changes (God's) character. What is true in the light is also true in the dark." Indeed, amidst both good times and bad, kids need to learn how they too can discover their unique God-given character.

For example, although my dad is the most giving, humble man I know, something kept me from passing down his character – we're different. Dad's a "what" guy who does what's right every time, but I'm all about why. And Dad rarely explained why. I couldn't copy Dad's character. I had to discover my own.

How would your kids' futures be molded if your passions and purpose determined your calendar, spending, and best efforts? They'd be prepared to choose godly character qualities and live them. And they'd be prepared to trust God and want to, whether standing in awe or kneeling in desperation.

In the next four chapters, the 1-2-3-U framework helps you discover the character to live your chosen qualities with integrity – one treasure of fulfillment, two forces of success, three choices of significance, and the real you – where you really are in fifteen well-done character traits. Then Chapter 12 makes a culture of character practical and fun by becoming a Character Hero who flavors your family with a secret sauce of character qualities.

Choices to practice:

1. What was a time of crisis in which you had to trust fuller?

2. Would you follow you? How could you lead yourself better?

3. What character qualities do you want to pass down to your kids?

Note: The 1-2-3-U Discovery exercise is also available in the free Workbook at www.timalba.com. You can print copies for each member of your family, church small group, or work team, and then review your individual assessments together. It's a memory you'll likely never forget.

Chapter 8

One Treasure of Fulfillment

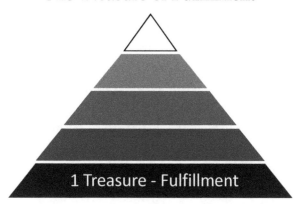

1 Treasure - Fulfillment

Like little Ralphie's Red Rider BB gun in the movie *A Christmas Story*, we've all had treasures that capture our imagination. After the excitement wanes, though, the reality of these treasures often doesn't measure up. Although these treasures won't "shoot your eye out," they fade over time like a BB gun. But not life's greatest treasures. Timeless treasures fulfill our souls for a lifetime as long as we keep pursuing them. That's God's plan for us – to be treasure hunters who don't give up as we grow up.

Matthew 13:44 states, "The kingdom of heaven is like a treasure hidden in the field, which a man found and hid; and from joy over it he goes and sells all that he has and buys that field." So too, in the Sermon on the Mount, Jesus offered something far greater than earthly treasure:

> Do not store up for yourselves treasures on earth, where moth and rust destroy, and where thieves break in and steal. But store up for yourselves treasures in heaven,

where neither moth nor rust destroys, and where thieves do not break in or steal; for where your treasure is, there your heart will be also" (Matthew 6:19-21).

Although curiosity seekers dominated that crowd, Jesus led a remnant to pursue what matters most. And that remnant changed the world. By aligning their passions with His, He chiseled their passions into fulfilling treasures.

In *What Matters Most*, Hyrum Smith writes, "When you discover what really matters most, you don't need to pretend or compare yourself with anyone else. You can start being yourself in the truest sense of the phrase." Your truest sense – your character – becomes a fulfilling treasure when it's lived with integrity every single day.

Having fulfilling treasures is one thing. Leading your family to want them too is something else. Kids need to see both humility and conviction in order to connect our character with theirs. This clicked for me one day while preparing my son for an interview. He was struggling with how to approach the interviewer. He asked, "Dad, should I be humble or confident?" I replied, "Son, you're asking the wrong question. You need both: be humble and act like you belong." As I've been learning in the years since, the path to faithfulness is also best seen through the dual lens of humility and conviction – "passion bifocals" that help us see life clearly.

Passion bifocals
I know, I know. Once you think you're humble, you're not. Humility is pursued, not possessed. But humility alone doesn't fulfill. Being humble needs to be balanced with conviction – acting like you belong. If humility exceeds conviction, you're aiming too low, never living up to your God-given potential. However, if conviction exceeds humility, you're overconfident, aloof, or presumptive. Either imbalance misses the mark.

Humble-conviction fuels faithfulness. It fueled the Apostle Paul to see himself as the chief of sinners, as well as someone to be imitated (1 Timothy 1:15, 1 Corinthians 11:1). Neither wimpy nor cocky, Paul lived with passion bifocals, as can you. You may not change the world like Paul, but your humble-conviction can change your world and generations to come.

Earlier, we used purpose bifocals to see One Purpose. Now, let's flip that over with passion bifocals to discover a passion that fulfills your purpose – your One Fulfilling Treasure.

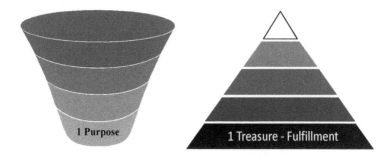

Purpose is what you're called to do; passion is what you're compelled to do. If God gives you a purpose, He'll surely give you a passion to fulfill it. But you have to discover it and build upon it. In upcoming chapters, you'll see how to invest purpose and passion in loved ones by first investing in you. Let's focus first on discovering your driving passion.

For decades, my six-word passion was: to hear Him say, "Well done!" Regardless of the situation or life stage, my driving passion remained unchanged. When God called me from corporate board rooms to ministry prayer rooms, I found a new outlet, not a new passion. In writing this book, however, I realized I was missing the point. I was missing the most important six words. These additional six words were surprisingly simple, yet life changing: "and help others do the same." Turns out, I had been too focused on me and didn't know it. Flipping my passion over to focus on others unleashed a whole new joy in fulfilling my purpose. Now my driving passion is twelve words: to hear Him say, 'Well done!" and help others do the same.

In 50-20-5-1, you chose Five Passions and One Purpose. Now in Step 1 of 1-2-3-U, you'll go further with a driving passion to fulfill your driving purpose. For example, here's how my Five Passions helped me discover my one fulfilling treasure.

<u>**Five Passions I live for**</u>   ("I'm fulfilled when I . . .")
1 Hear God say, "Well done!"
2 Faithfully fulfill my God-given Purpose
3 Lead my family/others to choose wisely & never forget why
4 Love Anna (which flows to my kids)
5 Passionately pursue excellence with integrity

<u>**One Fulfilling Treasure**</u>   (a driving passion):
To hear Him say, "Well done!" and help others do the same

Fulfilling treasures are your rock and hope. It's what you talk about without intending to. My kids surely got tired of hearing about well done because I talk about it all the time. But it slowly soaked in. They don't use the same words as me because they have their own passions, but each child slowly began talking about their own as they began discovering it.

Now it's your turn. What fulfills you because it fully fills you? What's in your gut, on the tip of your tongue, and pouring out of your life? Unlike Ralphie's BB gun, what sustains you for a lifetime, not just for a season? Are you grabbing it now, or is a crisis needed for it to grab you?

Someone who didn't wait for a crisis to grab his treasure is Steve Scheibner, a pilot who got bumped from a fatal 9-11 flight. Years earlier, Steve had declared his passion in a life objective: "To seek, trust, and glorify God through humble service and continual prayer. To raise up qualified disciples as quickly as possible. So that one day I might hear God say, 'Well done, my good and faithful servant!'" In his video, *In My Seat – A Pilot's Story from Sept 10th – 11th*, Steve says:

> The events of September 11th took that life objective that I already had, and it intensified it for me. The fire just keeps getting hotter as I get older. But some day, I want to stand in the Lord's presence and I want Him to say, "Well done!" I would hate to get in God's presence and have Him say, "Oh yeah, Scheibner, I see your name's down here. Well, have a seat." I need to hear the Lord say, "Well done, my good and faithful servant." That's what's on my plate and that's what's driving me these days.

What's driving you these days? Will it take a crash to put a life objective on your plate? Or will you do what Steve's video says, "Live like I'm on borrowed time" and discover a fulfilling what that inspires your family to a fulfilling life? That's what Jacob learned the hard way.

Fulfilling what

Jacob had to wrestle with God to discover his fulfilling what, and everything changed, even his name, Israel – "wrestle with God" (Genesis 32:28). Living with a fulfilling what makes life vividly real and personal. And it stays fresh, as the Holy Spirit renews you (2 Corinthians 3:17). Renewing is God's job; yours is being faithful whether life feels like a lovely spring or frigid winter.

Some people want life and parenting to be like Hawaii weather, where today is just like every seven-day forecast. When I asked Anna if she could live in Hawaii, she replied, "No, I need a change in climate." Indeed, we may want predictable paradise, but we need the challenge of change in order to live with God-given passion.

A God-given passion, though, isn't just for you. God gives you a passion that is the answer to other people's prayers. Therefore, *you* are the answer to someone's prayers, if you'll align with the passion God birthed in you. Are you using it to be that answer? Families, friends, and even strangers are waiting, hoping, praying for you to bless them, even if they don't understand it. They become open to their own treasures when they see it in you.

Do you know your One Fulfilling Treasure? Paul knew his – being "a light to the Gentiles" (Acts 13:47) to "open their eyes" (Acts 26:18). Not just a missionary, he was on a mission: "I have become all things to all people so that I may by all means save some" (1 Corinthians 9:22).

God gives you a treasure because He treasures you. He wants to live in you and stand by you. He wants faithfulness from you, fulfillment for you, and intimacy with you. Then you too can find your stone, just like the two exodus heroes, Joshua and Caleb.

What's Your Stone?

I named my sons Joshua and Caleb because of two exodus heroes who stood for God when others would not. No giant enemy or wimpy friend could deter their passion, which is what I wanted for my sons.

After crossing the Jordan River, Joshua erected a twelve-stone memorial, one stone for each of the twelve tribes, as a testimony for when their kids would ask, "What do these stones mean to you?" (Joshua 4:6). These twelve monuments proclaimed victory before it was attempted, and later proved that God keeps His promises.

After conquering the Promised Land, though, Joshua did something different. He set a large stone "under the oak that was by the sanctuary of the Lord. Then Joshua said to all the people, 'Behold, this stone shall be a witness . . . against you, so that you do not deny your God'" (Joshua 24:26-27).

Did Joshua use twelve stones again to commemorate final victory? No. Just one. Twelve tribes had become one nation. Many passions had become one fulfilling treasure. Joshua knew his stone – God – and he led his nation to choose it. By putting just one stone by the sanctuary, everyone was routinely reminded that God was their one stone. And still is.

What's your stone – your fulfilling treasure? Whatever it is, don't give up on it as you grow up. Know it. Pray it. Plan it. Live it. Build upon it. If you will, future generations can know theirs, and they'll never be the same.

But what if you lose everything? What's left? In *Man's Search for Meaning*, Dr. Viktor Frankl, a Nazi concentration camp survivor, says that when stripped to your bare nakedness, you still have the ability to choose. Frankl chose his response when other prisoners surrendered theirs. He lost his family and possessions, but the Nazis couldn't take his stone – his ability to choose.

You don't have to endure Frankl's trials to embrace his testimony. What choices shape your family legacy? Especially during tough parenting seasons, I've had to cling to the twelve words and exclamation point of my fulfilling treasure, because my goal isn't a nod of acceptance into heaven. I want my family to embrace a Savior who is excited to embrace us. I want to live with an exclamation point so that He uses one when saying, "Well done!" Periods satisfy; exclamation points fulfill. And only God's exclamation point will do!

What's your fulfilling treasure? If you can't clearly articulate it, it's hard to share it and pass it down. You can refine it over time, but take a moment now to write what you think it might be.

Discovering your one fulfilling treasure is just the first step of character that puts kids on the path to faithfulness. Character must become real and personal to kids too. Every what needs a how. In the next chapter, we'll progress up the 1-2-3-U Discovery pyramid of timeless character by building on a fulfilling passion with two forces of success. By aligning these two forces, you'll be compelled to not give up, to keep searching for the hidden treasures that can change eternity for you and the people you love.

Choices to practice:

1. How would your family describe your driving passion?

2. Humility and conviction – Which is more challenging for you and why?

3. How could you passionately live with an exclamation point?

Chapter 9

Two Forces of Success

What childhood memories warm your heart and stir your senses? I loved visiting grandparents, opening Christmas presents, and playing catch with Dad. Ah, but nothing topped Mom's cooking. I'd run home, fling open the door, and bask in the aroma of Mom's enchiladas. Her enchiladas symbolize a special bond between a mom and her son, as well as something greater than food recipes – success-determining character traits called "family recipes."

Family recipes, like food recipes, get passed down to future generations. My dad embraced an ideal for me, while my mom simply embraced me. Both passed down their own family recipe of love. Many of my kids' habits, as well as their favorite meals, are the same as mine. And when my young kids repeated one of my not-so-great phrases, they were extending my bad family recipes. Bad recipes require no special effort. By default, they continue for generations (Exodus 34:7).

Good family recipes, though, require more to continue – things like prayer, patience, and clear communication. Unless you articulate your good family recipes, they stop with you. Mom's enchilada recipe is an example. Since Mom didn't write it down, no one could replicate it until Anna wrote the recipe while baking them with Mom. The result: both Caleb and I put these enchiladas in our Fifty Pursuits.

What successful character traits of yours are your kids copying? They'll likely copy your character if you'll live like it really matters and like you really mean it. That's what Esther and Mary did. Esther risked her life to save her nation. Mary anointed Jesus' feet with perfume costing a year's wage. Neither was perfect, but both modeled the One who is. Multi-generational success, though, requires more than good role models; it also needs an effective plan.

Many parents are like the 100,000 unsuccessful Alaskan gold rushers in the 1890's – dreamers without a plan. They mean well. They try hard. They're committed. But their treasures stay lost because they're unprepared for a long, rocky journey. Following their hearts, they pursue fulfilling whats, yet flounder without a proven recipe of successful hows.

Successful Hows

Successful recipes don't guarantee success, but not using one virtually guarantees failure. So too, well-done parenting won't guarantee success, but default parenting virtually guarantees failure. Successful recipes bake in two successful hows – purpose and passion – the two driving forces that put your kids on the path to faithfulness.

1st driving force: Purpose

Purpose, the first driving force of success, is focused thinking – how you think and why you think that way. It's the cause propelling your effect. Purpose is what's way down deep inside – your guiding compass and unrelenting standard. It's what you would die for and won't live without because it's integral to everything and your integrity in everything.

Purpose is your boldness amidst apathy and calm during storms; your reasoning soul and sole reason; your last stand and life stance. It's the determination that drives you to become a driving force. It's the line you won't cross and, for Christians, it's Jesus' cross that takes you over the line.

Purpose is a what with a way for a why producing a wow. Colossians 3:23-24a puts it this way: "Whatever you do, do your work heartily, as for the Lord and not for people, knowing that it is from the Lord that you will receive the reward of the inheritance." Working is the what. Heartily is the way. And when God is the why, wow is the result.

You can try to copy someone else's purpose, but it won't fulfill your own. You may even choose a purpose, but purpose finds you when you seek it like hidden treasure. Purpose, though, is just the first half of the two driving forces of success. The second is passion.

2nd driving force: Passion

Whereas purpose is focused thinking, passion is focused action – how you act and why you act that way. Purpose fills you up; passion fires you up.

Passion is the burning desire that doesn't burn up or burn out, and why you pass up the good to pass along the great. It's why you love the unlovely, believe the unbelievable, and forgive 70 x 7 times without keeping score.

Passion surrenders your dreams without giving up on them. It's your unconditional tenacity, no-matter-what, and never-say-die. It's your "oh no, I will not" when tempted to fall and your "oh yes, I will" when challenged to rise. Passion isn't a favor exchanged; it's a privilege offered. It fuels you to go the extra mile with courage to take the next step. Passion is proof.

Passion also amazes for what it's not – conventional wisdom. Passion doesn't rely upon yesterday's victory for today's joy. It doesn't get pulled along, drift with the wind, or do the same ol' thing in the same ol' way and hope for better. It doesn't flip flop or fade; it produces faithful assurance, which produces fruitful action (Hebrews 11:1, Galatians 5:22-23). It doesn't just claim something matters; it has conviction to see it through.

Earlier, you were introduced to purpose bifocals and passion bifocals. They help you maximize your opportunity and be faithful today, along with being humble and acting like you belong. Together, purpose and passion yield something everyone wants – success. These two forces of success produce calculated clarity and fresh focus. A dream and a plan. A desired legacy and a directed path. They bond you with God and others.

Purpose is living like it really matters; passion, like you really mean it. Purpose gives direction and vision; passion, determination and vibrancy. Purpose fulfills; passion fuels. If aligned, they form the two sides of clear character. If they're misaligned, though, life is blurry. These two forces drive the success or failure of four groups of people.

Four groups of people

The charts below introduce these four groups of people based on four combinations of purpose and passion. Instead of putting you in a box, they'll help you see your life more clearly. (Later, we'll review the causes, characteristics, and consequences of all four ways of living.)

Group #1: Low Purpose & Low Passion

Some people lack purpose and passion. Small dreams and plans make them **victims** regardless of circumstances or environments.

Low
Purpose

Victim	

Low Passion is labeled at the row with **Victim**.

Group #2: High Purpose & Low Passion

Next are **regretful** people with more purpose than passion. They struggle with regret from not passionately pursuing their dreams. Focused thinking causes them to know better, but unfocused actions result in not doing better.

High
Purpose

	Regretful

Low Passion is labeled at the row with **Regretful**.

Group #3: Low Purpose & High Passion

Third are **busy** people with more passion than purpose, the opposite of group #2. They strive to do what others can't or won't do. Their problem isn't a lack of results; it's a lack of purpose.

Low
Purpose

Busy	

High Passion is labeled at the row with **Busy**.

Group #4: High Purpose & High Passion

Last are **successful** people who turn failure into success with high purpose and high passion. Success may not happen every time, but it's their pattern.

	High Purpose	
High Passion		**Successful**

This summarizes the four results of these two driving forces:

Low Purpose	x	Low Passion	=	**Victim**
High Purpose	x	Low Passion	=	**Regretful**
Low Purpose	x	High Passion	=	**Busy**
High Purpose	x	High Passion	=	**Successful**

Jesus described these four groups of people using four soils. He showed how your soil's fate depends on your soil's fertility.

The sower went out to sow (and) some seed fell beside the road, and the birds came and ate it up. And other seed fell on the rocky ground where it did not have much soil; and immediately it sprang up because it had no depth of soil. And after the sun had risen, it was scorched; and because it had no root, it withered away. And other seed fell among the thorns, and the thorns came up and choked it, and it yielded no crop. And other seeds fell into the good soil and as they grew up and increased, they yielded a crop and produced thirty, sixty, and a hundredfold (Mark 4:3-8).

Thorny	Good
Hardened	Rocky

Soil #1: Hardened

In Mark 4:14-20, Jesus interprets His parable, starting in verses 14-15 with hardened soil. "The sower sows the word. And these are the ones who are beside the road where the word is sown; and when they hear, immediately Satan comes and takes away the word which has been sown in them."

Low
Purpose

Hardened soils/souls	

Low Passion

Hardened soils are like emotionally compacted victims. Even the best seeds don't stand a chance on crusty surfaces. Showers of blessing run off instead of soaking deep inside. Biblical examples include: hard-hearted Pharaoh, who let the Jews exit Egypt only after God killed his first-born son; Pharisees, who rejected Jesus; and Judas, who betrayed Jesus.

We've all been hardened at times in different areas of life. How have you been hardened with low purpose and low passion?

Soil #2: Rocky

These are the ones on whom seed was sown on the rocky places, who, when they hear the word, immediately receive it with joy; and they have no firm root in themselves, but are only temporary; then, when affliction or persecution arises because of the word, immediately they fall away (Mark 4:16-17).

	High Purpose
Low Passion		**Rocky** soils/souls

Ground loosens, seeds are planted, and growth appears. Great times are ahead, right? Not when you're rocky and rootless. Without roots, there's no sustained growth or joy. Sowing more seeds isn't the answer. The answer is removing the rocks – competition, procrastination, distractions, or whatever crowds out your treasured seeds.

Rocky soils represent regretful people with more purpose than passion. Even if they're aware of their rocks, the rocks crowd out their passions. Then again, we often overlook our rocks, because it's easier to spot someone else's speck than to see our own boulders (Matthew 7:3-5).

For example, Saul knew better but didn't do better (1 & 2 Samuel). Achan hid forbidden treasures in his tent because they crowed out his heart (Joshua 7). John Mark left Paul and Barnabas on a missionary journey due to lack of roots (Acts 15:36-40). How have you too been rocky soil at times?

Soil #3: Thorny

And others are the ones on whom seed was sown among the thorns; these are the ones who have heard the word, and the worries of the world, and the deceitfulness of riches, and the desires for other things enter in and choke the word, and it becomes unfruitful (Mark 4:18-19).

Low
Purpose

High Passion	**Thorny** soils/souls	

Worries, wealth, and wonders – life thorns – silently blend in, choke, and keep you busy in survival mode. Since you can't kill everything, thorns grow until they're obvious (Matthew 13:24-43), and you have to address them. Thorns win by default by popping up in hard-to-reach places. Still, thorns are better than being hardened or rocky, right? No. The appearance of growth may look good for a while, but thorns eventually get exposed for what they are. A better plan is preventing them from taking root.

Thorny, busy biblical characters include: Martha, who was too busy serving Jesus to embrace him; the prodigal son's brother, who busily served his father but resented his brother's return; and the rich young ruler, whose love of money choked out Jesus' greater gift. In what ways have you been thorny soil?

Soil #4: Good

Jesus concludes in Mark 4:20: "And those are the ones on whom seeds were sown on the good soil; and they hear the word and accept it, and bear fruit, thirty, sixty, and a hundredfold."

High
Purpose

High Passion		**Good** soils/souls

The Bible is full of people with good soil. Some were famous like Esther. Some like Job were rich. Simeon, though was an ordinary guy who miraculously saw what others did not – the Messiah who had come as a baby (Luke 2:25-35).

Who do you know with good soil? I've had mentors like Dean Smith and Charlie Klaassen, encouragers like Don O'Neal and Jack Terrell, role models like Dianna Booher and Charles Thornton, franchisees like Tommy Marlin and Mike Tolleson, catalysts like Vernon Rae and Bill Anderson, and servants like Steve LaMar, Brian Nelson, and Gary Phillips. All get hardened, rocky, and thorny at times too, but they keep my soil fertile by cultivating theirs.

Whether your potential is thirty, sixty, or a hundredfold, God wants you to have fertile soil that grows a harvest and fulfills His purpose. A great example is Bob Buford, whose life goal was: "100x." In his life-changing book *Halftime*, Bob said he wants to be "the seed that was planted in good soil and multiplied a hundred fold. It is how I wish to live. It is how I attempt to express my passions and my core commitments (and) my legacy."

Thankfully, God sows seeds in us, even if our harvest isn't 100x. In fact, He often uses hardened, rocky, and thorny people to do His greatest work. He sowed seeds two millennia ago in twelve apostles with sub-standard soils, just like He does today with ordinary people like us.

	Low Purpose	High Purpose
High Passion	**Busy**	**Good**
Low Passion	**Victim**	**Regretful**

Here's a quick application. Write the names of people in the Bible and people you know who fit these four soil types. One biblical example is listed for each soil to get you started.

Victim /	Regretful /	Busy /	Successful /
Hardened	Rocky	Thorny	Good

People in the Bible:

Pharaoh	King Saul	Martha	Esther
_____	_____	_____	_____
_____	_____	_____	_____

People you know:

_____	_____	_____	_____
_____	_____	_____	_____

Where is your soil the best? Where does it need help? How has it changed over time? Even the best soils change. No one is good soil all the time. You too have surely ridden the rollercoaster of different soils in different areas because even Simon Peter and David, got hardened, rocky, and thorny.

Simon Peter's soil

Hardened Simon Peter – After saying he'd never deny Jesus, Simon Peter did so three times (Luke 22:54-62). You and I also get compacted, but God can still produce a harvest through us.

Rocky Simon Peter – Paul opposed Simon Peter when he buckled under peer pressure and withdrew from the gentiles (Galatians 2:11-14). We all lose passion for God when distracted from the God of our passion.

Thorny Simon Peter – Passion got him out of the boat to walk on water, but he sank when fear flooded his purpose (Matthew 12:22-33). Simon Peter too got stuck in the weeds when his passion ran ahead of his purpose.

Good Simon Peter — He healed the sick, preached at Pentecost, wrote epistles, and led the first century church. Jesus even changed Simon's name to Peter (rock). We'll never be Simon Peter, but we too can have a harvest grown in good soil by fulfilling the ministry God gives us.

David's Soil

Good David (2 Samuel 10:17-19) David led his army to victory, killing 700 charioteers, 40,000 horsemen, and the enemy's leader.

Rocky David (2 Samuel 11:1) Then David got complacent. Rather than going to battle with his army, he sent others and stayed home. Even a little complacency leads to regretful thoughts, behaviors, and consequences.

Hardened David (2 Samuel 11:2-5). When complacency knocked, tragedy answered — David impregnated Bathsheba. Slippery slopes inevitably lead to the underbelly of sin.

Thorny David (2 Samuel 11:6-13) David tried to hide his sin by recalling Uriah (her husband) from battle to sleep with Bathsheba. Passion to protect his throne overtook his purpose to advance God's throne.

Hardened David (2 Samuel 11:14-27) Things went from bad to worse. The man after God's heart murdered Uriah. David's for-whom reverted to himself, and he reaped what he sowed.

Good David (2 Samuel 12:1-12) David repented when confronted. Although David's child died, Bathsheba later bore David a wise successor king – Solomon. Then again, God loves cultivating failures for His glory. He sees them as pictures of possibilities, not photos of failures.

Four parents. Four kids.

The four kinds of soils produce four kinds of parents who, in turn, produce four kinds of kids. Sure enough, kids tend to be like their parents. If you're a hardened parent, you'll likely raise hardened kids. If a rocky parent, get ready for rocky kids. If you're thorny, expect thorny kids. And if you're good-soiled, your kids have a much greater chance of having 30, 60, or 100x harvests.

Although kids choose for themselves, the fate of their souls originates in the fertility of your soil. Therefore, one of the best gifts you can give your kids is to prepare your own soil.

In our parenting classes, Anna and I encourage struggling parents with this: don't take too much credit when your kids do great, and don't take too much blame when they don't. You can put faithfulness on a tee, but only they can whack it. Still, I've learned that kids are often like their parents on steroids, taking our good and bad qualities to extremes. Where they're thorny or rocky, we've often contributed. If we'll dig deeper into our kids' soils, we'll likely learn a lot about our own.

That's why marriage and parenting should be your primary ministries. Yes, Proverbs 22:6 says to train up a child in the way he should go and he won't depart from it when he's old. But that's a principle, not a promise. For example, the father in Luke 15 had both a faithful son and a prodigal son. Jesus had eleven good apostles and Judas. Many faithful parents have both godly and ungodly kids, despite similar parenting.

Your loved ones don't prove your faithfulness, but collectively they're indicators. If you look at your kids and those you influence, what do you tend to see? People with hardened, rocky, or thorny soils? Or do you see successful harvests grown from good soil? We all want success, but timeless character asks a fundamental question: "Success in what?"

Success in What?
In the spring of 1993, this became vividly real to me. I was on top of the world. Anna was pregnant with our third child. I had written a personal mission statement called *I Choose To*. As our company's youngest manager, I was featured in *Leaders*, a

company publication, with an article they entitled, *I Choose to ... Values that Work*. I was accomplishing goals and loving it. Maybe loving it a little too much. And although my motto was "content, but never satisfied," something was missing.

I had to relearn a hard lesson: success isn't enough. I wondered: *Is that all there is? Why does success feel empty?* What I didn't know was that God was preparing me for a season of utter desperation and dependence upon Him. In less than six months, my son was born and nearly died, Dad got cancer, Grandma died, my employer was sold, my job changed, and more.

Naturally, I asked God, "Why me?" Through those storms, though, He taught me to exchange my "why me?" of doubt with whys of faith. I saw how with each dark day, there's light. With each trial, there's joy. With each stumble, hope. And with each success, a new challenge.

Fast forward a decade. Despite bumps along the road, a few people at least said I was inspiring. Deserved or not, this new "success" can feel good. Maybe a little too good. As we'll see in the next chapter, being inspirational for others is better than being successful for yourself, but inspiring people also end up asking: *Is that all there is?*

Thankfully, there's something greater than inspiration and success. There's faithfulness. Faithfully fulfilling your purpose glorifies God. Even Jesus glorified God by faithfully fulfilling what His Father gave Him to do (John 17:4). Glorifying God is the end and faithfulness is the joyful means.

God measures success not by the comparability of your accomplishments, but by the completeness of your faithfulness. Even if you're not accomplished, you can faithfully cultivate good soil that makes it easy for your kids to grow a harvest.

If only we could see how our faithful soil helps so many people. For example, my kids and thousands of others are beneficiaries of my grandparents' good soil. Grandpa Loyd was a welder. Grandma Soledad was a Mexican housewife who never spoke English. Neither could have imagined how their faithfulness affected eternity.

Faithful legacies start with faithful families, but they don't stop there. When faithfulness is pursued like hidden treasure, God cracks open your cocoons of concern, birthing a whole new family. I now realize that you are part of *my* family because you're part of *God's* family – my "adopted" family. I choose you. We're kin, not through biology, but because God chose us. Therefore, how can I do anything but embrace you, my fellow adoptee?

In his book *Grace*, Max Lucado explains it from God's perspective: "My child, I want you in my new kingdom. I have swept away your offenses like the morning clouds. Your sins like the morning mist. I have redeemed you. The transaction is sealed; the matter is settled. I, God, have made my choice. I choose you to be part of my forever family."

In the next chapter, you'll discover the next step of 1-2-3-U. Step 3 shows how success yields significance when you whet the spiritual appetite of your family and adopted family. Those are the flavorful family recipes that let you bask in the sweet aroma of God's favor.

Choices to practice:

1. What family recipes (good and bad) have been passed down to you?

2. Is your life soil mainly hardened, rocky, thorny, or good? How about your kids' soil?

3. How have you been each soil? What caused it to change?

Chapter 10

Three Choices of Significance

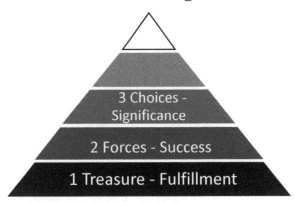

3 Choices - Significance

2 Forces - Success

1 Treasure - Fulfillment

No one expected much from Susanna, the youngest of twenty-five children and the unassuming wife of an impoverished preacher. Her life was spent loving and educating her nineteen kids. Susanna didn't preach sermons, write hymns, or lead a movement. She did nothing dramatic. But centuries later, Susanna Wesley is still a British hero for one reason: her legacy as a faithful mom. She changed the world through her kids, especially in the sermons and hymn lyrics of her sons, John and Charles Wesley. We, like Susanna, need to learn our true significance as parents – kids are the expression of our identity, not the source.

Everyone has a legacy, but are you choosing your legacy, or is any ol' legacy choosing you? Your greatest legacy isn't your passion or success; it's the significance of your character. My dad's legacy is humble service. Paul Kimball's is sacrificing his dreams and receiving a grander dream. Susanna Wesley changed the world as a mom. The Apostle Paul was an evangelist, pastor, and mentor. All of them passed down their timeless character to others who did the same. Another legacy maker is Dr. James Dobson, founder of Focus on the Family. In *Your Legacy: The Greatest Gift*, Dr. Dobson captures the significance of putting future generations on the path to faithfulness:

> For parents who believe passionately in Jesus Christ and anticipate His promised gift of eternal life, there is no higher priority in life than providing effective spiritual training at home. Unless we are successful in introducing our children to Him, we will never see them again in the afterlife. Everything else is of lesser priority.

We desperately want our kids to be Christ-followers, but our legacy as parents isn't based on our kids' faith. We can't make them follow Christ. Our legacy, which greatly influences our kids, is based on the significance of the person we strive to please – our "significant for-whom."

Significant for-whom
Fulfilling whats (one fulfilling treasure) and successful hows (two forces of success) are crucial, but they're not enough. "Success in what?" begs an even greater question: "Success for whom?"

The prior chapter introduced four groups – victims, regretful, busy, and successful – based on their purpose and passion. This chapter focuses on the successful group (high purpose and passion) and explores three progressive choices that determine the significance of their success. Here's the first of these three choices of significance:

<u>**Significance Choice #1:**</u>
**Will you live for YOUR purpose
and YOUR passion?**

When you live for your purpose and passion, success becomes the norm. This isn't just something you do; it's *you* because you're bought in, sold out, and fired up. Living for your purpose and passion isn't striving to hear, "Well done, *mediocre* servant." It's not doing mediocre work at a mediocre job, driving to a mediocre home, hugging a mediocre spouse, playing with mediocre kids, praying to a mediocre god, eating mediocre food, and one day having mediocre friends stand over a mediocre tombstone engraved, "Here lies Bob. He was mediocre."

Mediocre legacies often result from successful parents not applying their success principles at home. Although a revered prophet, Samuel let his promiscuous sons desecrate the temple (1 Samuel 8). How could Samuel be so faithful, yet his sons fail so miserably? It's because his purpose and passion were clear to his nation, but not to his kids. Like many parents, Samuel allowed sin at home that he wouldn't tolerate elsewhere.

Living for your purpose and passion is the foundation of Admirers – people who spawn success through clear, principled character. Their deeply-rooted purpose and far-reaching passion are admired by others, and they find admirable qualities in others. We love Admirers who motivate us to see what we can do.

	YOUR Purpose
YOUR Passion	Admirer

Admirers may not even be super-gifted, but they're super-engaged. Even if you don't love their cause, you admire their effect, which stems largely from two key characteristics: defining priorities and refining habits.

Most people make a living that defines their lives. Admirers, though, define priorities first and then live them. Their lives don't always match their dreams, but their priorities compel them to never stop pursuing those dreams. Admirers also refine habits like a refiner's fire. Their lesser habits burn away, leaving even clearer priorities. And although their lives get out of balance too, their "priority amnesia" is only temporary.

The problem with living for only your purpose and passion is that your for-whom – the person you're mainly blessing – is *you*. It happens subtly, as you unknowingly pursue your natural state – you. For years, I copied Admirers until realizing that relatively few of them have that "something more" of significance. I know because I've experienced success and thought, *There has to be something more.*

Have you ever wondered why success isn't what you expected? If so, God has something greater for you. In addition to saying yes to the first choice of significance – living for your purpose and your passion – God also wants your yes to the second choice of significance:

Significance Choice #2:
Will you live for a HIGHER purpose
and a HIGHER passion?

Sadly, my default is my family and me, as it probably is for you. But the grander why of choice #2 extends beyond the inward focus of choice #1. It's the gateway to an inspiring life lived for others.

More than an Admirer, you can be an Inspirer who inspires others with a higher purpose and higher passion. An Inspirer's for-whom is *others*, not themselves, which changes everything. A higher purpose and passion changes what you treasure because it changes who you treasure.

A HIGHER
Purpose

A HIGHER Passion		Inspirer

All Inspirers start out as Admirers, but few Admirers become Inspirers. I could list thousands of people I admire, but far fewer who also inspire. Inspirers serve people who don't appreciate it or reciprocate. They don't scratch your back so that you'll scratch theirs. And they share more than qualities and characteristics; they also share quality character.

Your purpose and passion are key, but they need to align with a higher purpose and passion. For example, how can you embrace a company's values without knowing yours? Knowing how you fit within a higher purpose isn't selfish. It's necessary and far more rewarding than living for you.

More than an Admirer who helps you see what you can do, Inspirers help you see who you want to be. Inspirers bless you by casting vision and crafting mission. Their vision isn't always new to you, but it always renews you. By continually casting their own vision, they inspire you to cast yours. Their stirring example spurs you to want to do the same.

Inspirers also craft a mission that connects the dots of life when life is dotted with disappointments. They work wonders in you because of the wonder of their works. And they help you believe you can too. Still, Inspirers face a reality check. I know because I've been there. I've sacrificed and served others with a higher purpose and passion, but I still got to a place of asking, *Why does success feel empty?*

Even higher purpose and passion feel hollow without something greater than you and others. This "something greater" kind of character is found in someone more, not something more. This someone is God – the third choice of significance that transforms and conforms you into the image of your for-whom Creator (Romans 12:2, 8:29):

Significance Choice #3:
Will you live for your GOD-GIVEN purpose and your GOD-HONORING passion?

Godly families live the right whats, hows, and whys, but they also point others to the right for-whom – the author and perfecter of faith, the rock of ages, the calmer of storms, the path straightener to the crooked, the hope instiller to the despondent, and the grace giver to the undeserving.

Don't try to initiate a relationship with God; just accept His standing offer. Don't try to meet God half way; He's already come to you. Don't try to shop for a better deal; He's already stamped "paid in full" on your sins to purchase your salvation. All He asks in return is that you live for your God-given purpose with God-honoring passion.

God-given purpose

Make no mistake, God-given purpose isn't any ol' purpose. Any ol' purpose is a mission; God-given purpose is more – it's a ministry. Any ol' purpose is a goal to accomplish; God-given purpose is a calling to fulfill. God invests His purpose in you and wants it back … with interest.

Bob Buford describes it this way in *Halftime:* "The stuff that stirs within the heart's holiest chamber is, I believe, a gift given to us all by our Creator." Buford continues, "It's a divine reminder that we are miraculously and wonderfully made in the image of God." Indeed, it enlightens even if today looks as dim as yesterday. It encourages dejected parents awaiting a prodigal's return. And like a maturing marriage, it grows sweeter each day.

There's a progression to God-given purpose. How you think frames your purpose, which inspires a higher purpose when it shifts to others. But nothing transforms like God-given purpose.

your purpose ⟶ a higher purpose ⟶ God-given purpose

God-honoring passion

So too, God-honoring passion isn't any ol' passion. Any ol' passion gratifies, but God-honoring passion also glorifies. Any ol' passion loves the people you love most; God-honoring passion loves the people you love least. The former achieves goals; the latter accelerates giftedness.

God-honoring passion has unending determination to realize God-given dreams. More than living before you die; it's dying to yourself so that you can truly live. It converts how you see, as evidenced by how you act. It multiplies your talents before laying them at Jesus' feet, rather than burying them (Matthew 25) or giving Him the lame and leftovers (Malachi 1).

There's also a progression leading to God-honoring passion. Action forges passion, which inspires a higher passion when you love others. But only God-honoring passion transforms the soul.

your passion ⟶ a higher passion ⟶ God-honoring passion

God liberally gives His purpose to you, and you cheerfully give God-honoring passion back to Him (2 Corinthians 9:7). This isn't a transaction or begrudging obligation; it's how you gladly thank Him in return. It's your way of regifting your God-given purpose for His glory and others' benefit.

God-given purpose draws you in; God-honoring passion drives you on. Aligned and balanced, they're both catalysts of

111

bonding faithfulness. Old things are passed away; all things become new (2 Corinthians 5:17). You see with a fresh view, live with a new vigor, and become an Aspirer.

	GOD-GIVEN Purpose	
GOD-HONORING Passion		Aspirer

Aspirers are those few people who are desperate for, tuned into, and driven by a God-birthed zeal to pass it on. They find significance by aligning God-given purpose with God-honoring passion. I appreciate Admirers and Inspirers who lift the veil shrouding our lives. But I cherish Aspirers who rip the veil in two.

Admirers help you see what you can do. Inspirers help you see who you want to be. But Aspirers help you become who you are created to be. They don't want you to copy them; they want to maximize the godly character within you because God is their for-whom.

Admirers $\longrightarrow$ Inspirers $\longrightarrow$ Aspirers

One of my favorite examples of this progression is Joe Croce, the ultra-successful founder of CiCi's Pizza. His laser-focused leadership turned a one-store pizza joint into a customer service phenomenon with millions of raving fans. Still, I witnessed a greater miracle than skyrocketing sales. I saw Joe transform into an Aspirer. With the gentle touch of his wife, Kimberly, Joe's success became measured by faithfulness, not financials. More than restaurants, Joe invested in people and eternity.

Then again, when your gaze shifts toward faithfulness, love flows from your character. Without love, we're nothing (1 Corinthians 13:2). Good intentions wither without intentional goodness. By serving their Creator, they serve their Creator's purpose. Aspirers share two additional key characteristics: surrendering destiny and fulfilling ministry.

Surrendering destiny & fulfilling ministry

Three of my career experiences illustrate how surrendering destiny is like peeling layers of an onion. First, my dream of working with Dr. Nathan Jones came true when he asked me to co-lead a start-up venture. In every detail, we saw God's confirmation as the deal came together. I had never been more certain of God's direction, so I stepped out in faith and quit my job. Three days later, the phone rang at 2:30 a.m. It was Nathan telling me that the funding fell through and the deal was dead.

At that moment, the deal wasn't the only thing that died. My dream also died. Crushed and numb, I collapsed, asking how I could have been so wrong. In utter despair, I realized something I had never considered: I hadn't yet surrendered my career to God … all of it, especially the most cherished parts. As it turns out, though, that was just the first layer of surrendering my destiny.

The second layer peeled off seven years later during a management-led buyout of CiCi's. I had worked 80+ hours per week for nearly a year and everything was finally coming together. Then it happened again. My dear friend and boss, Forbes Anderson, pulled me aside and said the deal had died. With face buried in my hands, I sat in stunned silence, trying to do what I hadn't done since my career had seemingly died seven years earlier – cry. But I was too exhausted for tears, so I cried out: *Why, God? I sacrificed a year for this dream. How could I have been so wrong?*

In desperation, I came to a new realization. Although I had surrendered my life, family, career, and possessions, I hadn't surrendered my hopes and dreams. In brokenness, I released this last bastion of control. In the depths of despair, I realized that my for-whom was still me. I had to re-learn that God either makes dreams come true or He gives you new dreams. But the story doesn't end there.

Another seven years later, off came another layer. I had been blessed with my dream job as CFO and part-owner of CiCi's when the buyout got completed after all. Life was great. Then, out of nowhere, God called me to serve my church full time. Seriously? This wasn't on my agenda. But I had to keep a promise I had made God over twenty years earlier – that I would surrender anything if He ever called me to vocational ministry. Thus, I had to surrender my dream job too. And yet again, God uncovered a new layer of character that I could pass along to my kids: timeless significance requires agenda-less surrender.

In addition to surrendering destiny, we also need to fulfill ministry – God's ministry, not ours. Fulfilling ministry is an Aspirer's joy because it's their joyful calling. Once you've experienced it, nothing else satisfies. Thus, despite impending death in prison, Paul challenged his young Aspirer, Timothy, with these three words: "Fulfill your ministry" (2 Timothy 4:5).

First century Aspirers lived out their purpose and passion (choice #1). They left professions and donated possessions for a higher purpose and passion (choice #2). And they fulfilled a God-given calling with God-honoring passion even unto death (choice #3). But they first surrendered themselves completely, immediately, and sacrificially to God (2 Corinthians 8:5).

Fulfillment starts by personalizing, prioritizing, and perpetuating your God-given purpose. If you will, your For-Whom will pull you in close, wipe away your tears, and welcome you into heaven. To what has your For-Whom called you? Are you fulfilling it? Here's a summary of the three types of character enabled by the three choices of significance:

	#1 Admirer	#2 Inspirer	#3 Aspirer
Three Choices of Significance	Your Purpose & Your Passion	A Higher Purpose & A Higher Passion	God-given Purpose & God-honoring Passion
Blessing	You	Others	God
Focus	What & How	Why	For-Whom
Impact	Help us see what we can do	Help us see who we want to be	Help us become who we're created to be
Two Key Characteristics	Define priorities & Refine habits	Cast vision & Craft mission	Surrender destiny & Fulfill ministry

Who do you know that is an Admirer? An Inspirer? An Aspirer? Please take a moment to write their names below and then thank them, especially the Aspirers, who've helped you become who you're created to be.

Admirers: _____

Inspirers: _____

Aspirers: _____

What about you? Do people admire you? Do you inspire them to be like you? Or are you an Aspirer who helps people find significance by aspiring to be who God created them to be? It all depends on your for-whom. If, like Susanna Wesley, your for-whom is God, your kids can be the expression of your identity, not the source. By clinging to your identity in God, you empower your kids with the character to do the same, even when their actual path isn't their preferred path.

To be your family's Aspirer, though, you need to know your life soil. The next chapter, the last step of 1-2-3-U, helps you discover the real you – your soil type in fifteen well-done character traits – in order to be an Aspirer that puts your kids on the path to faithfulness.

Choices to practice:

1. Whose legacy of significance would you like to emulate?

2. Do you live primarily as an Admirer, Inspirer, or Aspirer?

3. How can you more fully surrender your destiny?

Chapter 11

The Real You (U)

"My two-year-old son is gone," screamed the mom. "He was right here! We have to find him NOW before it's too late!" Nothing grips your heart like a lost child. But do you to drop everything and leap into action? The answer is: It depends. When you don't know the child, you're empathetic but unlikely to act. When it's *your* child, though, everything changes. On Thanksgiving Day 1995, it was *my* child. And everything changed.

Like every Thanksgiving, the aromatic whiff of slow-cooking turkey engulfed the house. Cousins were playing and parents reminiscing. Then it happened. My two-year-old son, who never wandered off, was missing. And no one knew how long. We checked the usual hide-and-seek locations. Louder and louder, we called his name. Still, no answer. That's when reality struck and everyone froze, imagining the horrific possibilities.

Anna crumbled in the floor, weeping uncontrollably. Relatives scoured the neighborhood. I drove and drove, frantically yelling my son's name. Was he safe? Would I ever get to hold him again? One, and only one, thing mattered at that moment – saving my son.

After what felt like an eternity, we found him way down the street eating candy with a stranger! No questions asked. We just thanked them, snatched him up, and headed home. For hours, Anna clung to him and cried until she could cry no more, while I sat in stunned silence, pondering what might have been.

The rollercoaster of that day's emotions still grips my soul. I've never been more compelled because I've never been more desperate. I never again want to be driven to the brink of tragedy before I'm driven to my knees. I want to embrace what truly matters – my compelling treasures.

Too often, compelling treasures go missing. Desperation becomes routine. Priorities get overwhelmed. Opportunities go unnoticed. For example, if a revered leader invited you to a private meeting, would you go? The answer is: It depends. If you don't cherish the inviter, you won't cherish the invitation. So too, some people cherish God's invitation to join His family. Others rebuff. But an even more dangerous response is to defer.

> A man was giving a big dinner, and he invited many; and ... he sent his slave to tell those who had been invited, "Come; because everything is ready now." And yet they all alike began to make excuses... And the master said to the slave, "(Compel) them to come in, so that my house will be filled" (Luke 14:16-18, 23).

It's not that they would never attend. They had good excuses, but none justified rejecting the master's invitation. Before judging, though, let's look at ourselves. Do we ever get familiar or busy? Do days or weeks pass without intimacy with God and family? Likely yes. But that changes if we'll probe our character to ensure it puts our kids on the path to faithfulness.

As a young farm hand, I pushed a long metal probe in the ground, dumped dirt in a bag, and marked the bag. No big deal, right? Wrong. Although it meant nothing to me then, I later learned that farmers, like families, take samples to maximize their harvests. Satisfied people, though, have no need for samples. This chapter helps you take samples of your life soil to assess your character – your "authentic where" – where you really are in preparing for 30, 60, or 100x family harvests.

Authentic where
If only life came with a you-are-here map and directions. Since it doesn't, you need to know where you are in the process of growing fulfillment, success, and significance into fertile faithfulness. David asked God to search him and see where his heart really was (Psalm 139:23-24). Similarly, Step U of 1-2-3-U helps you assess where you really are like a you-are-here map of your character.

You'll also see in which areas you can become a more faithful you by probing fifteen well-done character traits and circling the soil type that best represents the real you in those traits. These fifteen traits fit within three areas of life: 1) life-sight, 2) life-style, and 3) life-call.

<u>Life-sight: What you see & why</u>
How's your eyesight? Without corrective lenses, everything looked fuzzy. But I didn't know that my sight had faded. I didn't know that colors were so bright or that classroom chalk boards weren't hazy to everyone. I needed correction, but didn't know it.

So too, how I see life – my life-sight – often needs correction. You too may not have 20/20 eyesight, but you can see circumstances with 20/20 character. The first five character traits – vision, lens, perspective, outlook, and focus – clarify what you see and why.

Trait #1: Vision

Vision is the character to see through circumstances. In *The Circle Maker,* Mark Batterson says life-changing prayer is what you pray through. As with prayer, vision drives your choices because it's what you believe is on the other side. What kind of vision rules your life? Here are four possibilities.

- First, is life a string of unending **pursuits** that rarely pan out or satisfy? If so, the reason your vision doesn't grab your soul may be because it's a bit cloudy with low purpose and low passion. You may have a Pursuits type of vision.

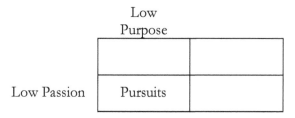

- Second, do you commonly juggle too many **priorities**? Purpose without matching passion causes regret because you don't see it through. If so, Priorities may characterize your vision with high purpose and low passion.

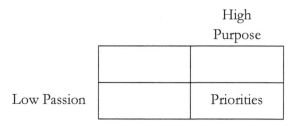

- Third, do you get routinely busy with **passions** that seem obvious to you but not to others? Zeal is great, unless it lacks matching purpose. If that's you, you may have a Passions vision with high passion and low purpose.

	Low Purpose	
High Passion	Passions	

- Finally, when God-given purpose and God-honoring passion align, you see life with compelling **Purpose**. Everyone needs occasional adjustments, but Purpose-vision people can see through circumstances without missing today's joy.

		High Purpose
High Passion		Purpose

Please circle the quadrant below that best reflects your vision. As you do the same for all fifteen well-done character traits below, you'll see where improving your life soil can improve your family.

	Low Purpose	High Purpose
High Passion	Passions	Purpose
Low Passion	Pursuits	Priorities

Trait #2: Lens

The second well-done character trait is your lens – how character adjusts to circumstances. Your life-sight, like a lens, can be corrected if diagnosed.

- Many people are **narrow sighted**. Do you typically see life in a narrow band of familiarity, not surrounding possibilities?

- **Far sighted** people look to the future, but miss what's up close. Do you tend to overlook the everyday treasures of life?

- Are you **near sighted**, seeing details but missing the bigger picture? It happens stealthily as life-sights change over time.

- No one sees clearly all the time, but is your lens normally **clear sighted**? The key isn't perfect sight; it's clarity to adjust.

Many of us need bifocals, literally and figuratively. Long before I needed bifocal eyeglasses, I kept an old pair of bifocals at my desk as a symbolic reminder to look for both the big picture and the details in all areas of life. Thankfully, no matter what we see, God can correct our life lens if we'll ask Him. Please circle the box below that best represents your life lens.

	Low Purpose	High Purpose
High Passion	Near sighted	Clear sighted
Low Passion	Narrow sighted	Far sighted

Trait #3: Perspective

Perspective goes beyond vision (seeing through circumstances) and lens (adjusting to circumstances). It's how your character internalizes circumstances. Here is how purpose and passion can affect your perspective.

- Do you often feel **deprived**? Is life unfair? Do you want to be someone else with more advantages than you?
- Do you find yourself trying to **survive**? Do circumstances wear you down and prevent you from mustering up the gumption to prosper?
- Do you **strive** non-stop for another goal, prize, or relationship? Do you overcome and give your utmost, but not always for His highest?
- Or do you **thrive** in good times and bad? Yes, you struggle sometimes, but do circumstances bring you back to the privilege of serving God?

Which of these four internal perspectives is most like you? As with all of these fifteen well-done character traits, please circle the one most like you.

	Low Purpose	High Purpose
High Passion	Strive	Thrive
Low Passion	Deprive	Survive

Trait #4: Outlook

Whereas perspective is how character internalizes circumstances, outlook is its external expression – how character impacts others.

- Do your circumstances cause overwhelming **stress?** Everyone gets stressed, but do your struggles distress you and others you influence?

- Some people's outlook is intermittent. It's anyone's **guess.** Sometimes, their future looks great; other times, not. The inconsistency is draining to everyone involved.

- Is your motto: **press** on? It's great to persist when others fall away, but does constant pressure squeeze other people into your little box?

- Circumstances can also be character-revealing platforms to **bless** others. Do you inspire others to join you in becoming conduits of blessing?

Is your outlook stressing, guessing, pressing, or blessing?

	Low Purpose	High Purpose
High Passion	Pressing	Blessing
Low Passion	Stressing	Guessing

Trait #5: Focus

Even with a great vision, lens, perspective, and outlook, we all need focus – how character succeeds regardless of circumstances. People remember your character based largely on how well you stay true and focused during trials.

- Are you **resigned** to what you *can* see, not what you *could* see? Do you pull away quickly because it's hard to stay focused?

- Selling without risk of ownership is consignment. You can return it when you're done trying. Does your focus get **consigned**, because you won't risk much or you lose interest?

- Do you fulfill **assigned** tasks without feeling fulfilled? When juggle too many things, it's sadly the important ones that often get dropped.

- Or does your focus stay **aligned** on God with a balance of what He gave you to love and what He gave you to do?

	Low Purpose	High Purpose
High Passion	Assigned	Aligned
Low Passion	Resigned	Consigned

Life-style: How you live & why

Life-style is the evidence of character – what you do about your convictions. It's how you live and why. As a little boy, I imitated my dad by shaving with my little cardboard razor. As a parent, though, the tables turned, as my kids began imitating me. I saw our family character on display, based on how my kids were personalizing it. Sometimes that was great, like when Caleb washed dishes to bless his mother, Josh refused to accept his friend's excessive cursing, and Leslie gave me a CD about a girl who grew up watching her daddy's faithfulness. But I also saw the flip side – evidence of my hardened, rocky, and thorny soil – when my kids imitated my flaws.

You surely want to fix your character flaws, but you can't fix what you don't know. Therefore, here are five more traits to reveal the reality of your lifestyle: commitment, drive, workmanship, obstacles, and results.

Trait #6: Commitment

Commitment – the attachment to character – persists when circumstances tell you to walk away. Like a great marriage, commitment won't consider an exit strategy because you've pre-chosen your response when times get bad. How committed are you really to your greatest treasures?

- Do you live like a **member**? Many people in families, churches, and companies want to be a part, yet don't engage.

- Some people go further as **attenders**. They show up, but don't grow up because they'll concur with a cause, but rarely commit to it.

- Everyone loves **extenders** – human extension cords who connect to everything, but then get overloaded and unplug. Do you often get over extended?

- Rather than retreating from difficulties, others **surrender** fully, cheerfully, and liberally to their vows. Then again, they can't imagine any other way because they're dedicated.

	Low Purpose	High Purpose
High Passion	Extender	Surrender
Low Passion	Member	Attender

Trait #7: Drive

While commitment reflects attachment to character, drive keeps character intact. Drive is practical and active. It turns great intentions into a great reality. For example, many people are committed to getting into heaven, but far fewer are passionately driven to hear, "Well done!" upon arrival.

- Some people live like **renters**, not owners. As victims of problems, not victors of possibilities, they lack the drive to jump on opportunities.

- Others say, "I **meant** to do better, but __" and fill in the blank with good intentions. But meant well isn't well done.

- A **spent** life becomes obvious, but often after it's too late. Do you get caught up, maybe even obsessed, with your passions?

- Others don't just go; they feel **sent**. By trusting their Sender, they believe that no calling is too trivial, no sacrifice too great, and no dream too distant to faithfully fulfill it.

	Low Purpose	High Purpose
High Passion	Spent	Sent
Low Passion	Rent	Meant

Trait #8: Workmanship

Workmanship – the dutiful expression of character – gives you the credibility to lead. It's how and for whom you invest your time, money, and efforts.

- Some workers are **decoys** who look like the real deal, but unknowingly have become imitations of what they could be or used to be.

- Another type of worker is **no-joy**, someone who knows what you're capable of doing and becoming, but doesn't quite realize your potential.

- We all love to **employ** hard workers who meet expectations. But are you a hired hand, instead of taking ownership of your workmanship?

- Others are like soldiers (2 Timothy 1:18, 2:4), ready and eager to be **deployed** at a moment's notice. Their untangled workmanship is an offering to their Heavenly Commander.

	Low Purpose	High Purpose
High Passion	Employ	Deploy
Low Passion	Decoy	No-joy

Trait #9: Obstacles

Obstacles – opportunities to overcome obstructions to character – arise despite everything we do to prevent them. When financial ruin, spiritual deserts, emotional despair, or medical emergencies happen, our response reveals how we view those obstacles.

- Do your obstacles become insurmountable **blockades**? They can't be navigated if you feel blocked in without an escape.
- Obstacles can also be seen as **roadblocks** that inconvenience and require alternatives because you lose momentum, focus, and motivation.
- Some see obstacles as **stumbling blocks** that trip and keep you from your destination. If so, God can keep you from stumbling and present you blamelessly and joyfully before His glorious presence (Jude 24).
- Obstacles can also be **building blocks**. Corrie Ten Boom's Nazi concentration camp lessons touched millions. Nehemiah overcame naysayers to rebuild a wall and a nation. And Moses overcame a speech impediment to speak boldly to Pharaoh and a nation of millions. When God's agenda becomes yours, obstacles become building blocks of glory.

	Low Purpose	High Purpose
High Passion	Stumbling block	Building Block
Low Passion	Blockade	Roadblock

Trait #10: Results

Results are the bottom line – the effectiveness of character. God loves good commitment, drive, workmanship, and overcoming obstacles, but good enough is not well done. God wants us to win now, as well as win in heaven.

- Some people's poor results **restrain** others. As the CFO of CiCi's, our 100+ million annual guests loved our service, but even one weak link restrained hundreds of wows.

- Some **maintain** status quo. They're good, but rarely dare to be great. Then again, mediocrity in good times is often masked by good results.

- Others **attain** goals yet feel drained. Despite plenty of results, their challenge is staying mindful of why they strive so hard.

- Aspirers **sustain** results through the six words that eluded me for years – "and help others do the same." They develop skills but maximize their potential by developing others.

	Low Purpose	High Purpose
High Passion	Attain	Sustain
Low Passion	Restrain	Maintain

129

Life-call: Who you are & why

Building on what you see (life-sight) and how you live (lifestyle), a life-call is who you are, as revealed in how you relate to others, handle change, enjoy the journey, act in faith, and finish your race. It starts with choosing to fulfill God's calling for you.

This hit home for me one day at a job I felt compelled to do, but hated – selling Bibles door to door. One week, I sold only three Bibles. It wasn't for a lack of commitment, drive, or hard work. I was just a lousy salesman. After a month of utter defeat, I slumped down against a stop sign and begged God for courage. Too stubborn to quit, I faced a crossroad.

In debilitating fear, I randomly opened the Bible I was trying to sell and read Ephesians 4:1: "I, the prisoner of the Lord, implore you to walk in a manner worthy of the calling with which you have been called." It hit me: Would I be compelled by, or just compliant to, God's calling? In that moment, my life changed forever. In selling, I became my manager's recruiting example of how bad you can be before finding success. And in life, I began seeing God in the difficult seasons of His calling and, although it's never easy, I'm learning to thank Him for those seasons.

Have you ever just complied with God's calling? Please let these last five traits reveal if you're really embracing your calling.

Trait #11: Relationships

The first life-call trait is relationships – God's ultimate character builder. Relationships perpetuate faith, provide hope, and prove love. They comfort, heal, connect, and grow. God created mankind for a relationship with Him and sent His Son to restore it. He adores relationships, and so should we.

- Presumptive relationships are **depleting**. Like a snowball rolling downhill, they carve a wide path of destruction.

- Some relationships have **repeating** shortcomings. Same song, different verse. Love is exchanged like a transaction, not offered as a free gift.

- Are your relationships **competing**? Shallow relationships don't grow, especially with people who care more about what you do for them than about you.

- **Completing** relationships conquer weaknesses and reinforce strengths. Like Epaphras, their mature relationships complete God's will (Colossians 4:12). By becoming complete in Jesus, we can help others complete their relationships too.

	Low Purpose	High Purpose
High Passion	Competing	Completing
Low Passion	Depleting	Repeating

Trait #12: Change

Change reveals your conviction of character – whether change is liberating or debilitating. Too often, we try to avoid or endure change. Granted, not all change is good, but by embracing change that honors God, we release God to be our Change Agent.

- Resisting change can cause you to feel **deformed** and twisted into knots. If so, you may rust out or run aimlessly, with undesired results.

- Some are consumed with **informing**. But information without inspiration hardens hearts that wonder what's wrong with everyone else.

- Others are busy **reforming** their past into a new future. Reformation alone, though, doesn't heal unless it includes a character infusion.

- When God is **transforming** you, change becomes transforming like Romans 12:2: "(Keep on being) transformed by the renewing of your mind so that you may prove what the will of God is." That's ongoing, intentional change birthed from ongoing, intentional character.

	Low Purpose	High Purpose
High Passion	Reforming	Transforming
Low Passion	Deformed	Informing

Trait #13: The journey

Life journeys reveal the resiliency of character. Is your journey joyful and leading to a God-honoring destination? The exodus Jews wandered forty years in the wilderness because their purpose and passion kept wandering. But we can live in God's promised land by living in God's promised hand.

- Are you **rejecting** God's promises? Do you feel rejected? Either way you'll miss the joy of your journey.
- Are you **reverting** to the comfort of the good ol' days? Reverting is comforting, but it keeps you in the desert.
- Do you have **unrelenting** passion, charging ahead even if God says wait? We need obedience to His will, not passion for our preferences.
- The prize for **repenting** is intimacy with God. Repenting renews and connects us to God. His Son's sacrifice allows us to enjoy our earthly journey and our eternal destination if we're continually confessing and repenting (1 John 1:9).

	Low Purpose	High Purpose
High Passion	Unrelenting	Repenting
Low Passion	Rejecting	Reverting

Trait #14: Faith

Faith is evidence of character – how you walk, live, and love (2 Corinthians 5:7, Galatians 3:5, 1 Corinthians 13:2). It's the assurance of things hoped for (Hebrews 11:1) and a blessing with hope (Galatians 3:9, 26). God's grace opens heaven's door, but we walk through that door with faith (Ephesians 2:8-9). The question is not: What is faith? The question is: What is *your* faith?

- Some people are **pretending** to have faith. Like a convincing actor, they've learned to play the part. But faith is not a play.

- Although **intending** to take a leap of faith, many never dive in. Saving faith isn't just intellectual or emotional. It's intentional (James 2:14-16). But well intended isn't well done.

- Are you **depending** on you? It's natural but trying to save yourself is the futile path of all other religions.

- Godly faith is **contending** (Jude 3). We fight a real enemy. Before miraculously defeating his enemy, Gideon had to destroy alters to Baal. Then God called him Jerubbaal, "contend with Baal" (Judges 6:32).

	Low Purpose	High Purpose
High Passion	Depending	Contending
Low Passion	Pretending	Intending

Trait #15: Finish line

Imagine finishing your race and realizing that the other runners are nowhere to be seen. On earth and in heaven, here are four common character-caused possibilities.

- Many runners are **finished at the start**. They run but never stand a chance because they're going through the motions. False character.

- Some start strong but **fade at the finish.** They lack the training or the will to compete all the way to the finish line. Fading character.

- Others run hard, but **finish the wrong race**. Like Jim Marshall, a football player who ran the wrong way and scored for the wrong team, passion backfires when running to the wrong goal. Faulty character.

- A relatively few runners **finish strong**. In *Finishing Strong*, Steve Farrar explains why only one in ten young ministers are still on track at age sixty-five. Like Jesus, these few faithful soils will hear God say, "In you I am well pleased" (Mark 1:11, Luke 3:22). Faithful character.

	Low Purpose	High Purpose
High Passion	Finish the wrong race	Finish strong
Low Passion	"Finished" at the start	Fade at the finish

If we assess our own life soils, we're less likely to throw dirt on others. When accusers brought an alleged adulteress to Jesus in John 8:1-11, He had them take a sample of their own soils before casting the first stone.

Samples show us where to break up hardened places, remove rocks, and dig out weeds. And since all soils need cultivating, we need routine samples if we want our kids to inherit good soil. Please circle your soil for each of the fifteen well-done character traits below, or do so in the free Workbook at www.timalba.com.

LIFE-SIGHT: What you see & Why

Vision	Pursuits	Priorities	Passions	Purpose
Lens	Narrow sighted	Far sighted	Near sighted	Clear sighted
Perspective	Deprive	Survive	Strive	Thrive
Outlook	Stress	Guess	Press	Bless
Focus	Resign	Consign	Assign	Align

LIFE-STYLE: How you live & Why

Commitment	Member	Attender	Extender	Surrender
Drive	Rent	Meant	Spent	Sent
Workmanship	Decoy	No-joy	Employ	Deploy
Obstacles	Blockade	Roadblock	Stumbling block	Building block
Results	Restrain	Maintain	Attain	Sustain

LIFE-CALL: Who you are & Why

Relationships	Depleting	Repenting	Competing	Completing
Change	Deformed	Informing	Reforming	Transforming
The Journey	Rejecting	Reverting	Unrelenting	Repenting
Faith	Pretending	Intending	Depending	Contending
Finish Line	"Finished" at the start	Fade at the finish	Finish the wrong race	Finish strong

Please count how many of your answers are in each of the four columns and write that down for your Life-Sight, Life-Style, and Life-Call. Then total the four columns to better understand if you live primarily as a victim with hardened soil, regretful with rocky soil, busy with thorny soil, or an aspirer with good soil.

	Victim / Hardened	Regretful / Rocky	Busy / Thorny	Aspirer / Good	Total
Life-Sight	_____	_____	_____	_____	5
Life-Style	_____	_____	_____	_____	5
Life-Call	_____	_____	_____	_____	5
Total	_____	_____	_____	_____	15

Choose your soil. Choose your legacy.

By choosing your life soil, you choose your legacy because your soil becomes your kids' topsoil. No one wants kids to be victims, regretful, or busy, but it happens. Chances are, though, you also mix in some good soil – a desire to see clearer, live holier, and love purer. Which are you blending most into your kids – infertile soil or fulfilling soil? Infertile parents inhibit character. But fulfilling parents take samples of their own soils in order to maximize their kids' harvests.

Please don't miss the point, though, like I did for years. I treasured my choices and took samples of my character. I even tried to be a role model. But I had to shift from my preferences to what my kids needed in order to pass down my faith to them. Like the diagram below, I had reached a plateau, and so will you, if you (U) are on top.

Don't live plateaued. Live with a clear point that aligns with Jesus' last words: "But you will receive power when the Holy Spirit has come upon you; and you shall be My witnesses both in Jerusalem, and in all Judea and Samaria, and even to the remotest part of the earth" (Acts 1:8). Jesus' point: You're equipped now, so pass it on. Put others, not you, on top.

In the next chapter, you'll find practical ways of passing it on by making character fun and real with a secret sauce of family character qualities. You'll learn how to be a character hero that your kids and others can not only connect with, but also emulate in their own unique ways.

Choices to practice:

1. What story would a sample of your life soil tell?

2. Are you creating compliant kids or compelling kids?

3. Which of the 15 character traits has your best soil? The worst?

Chapter 12

Character Heroes

Did you know that Batman was from Iowa, not Gotham City? As a five-year-old, he prowled the yard in his Batman gloves, shoes, mask, and ultra-cool cape flapping in the breeze. He searched all day for villains until his two older sisters came home on the school bus. This little hero was quite muscular and brilliant too. Yes, that's my story, and I'm sticking to it! I wasn't playing Batman. I *was* Batman.

We love superheroes. We want to be just like them. They're smart and strong. They protect us and find a way, no matter what. They help us dream big dreams of who we can be. More than superheroes, though, kids need character heroes who instill character in them, speak character over them, and celebrate the character already within them. Character heroes mold a culture that kids can believe in now and want to copy decades later.

1-2-3-U provides a framework to live your chosen character qualities with integrity. This chapter provides practical tools to help kids become character heroes, starting with what kids can expect from you.

My dream as a young parent was that my kids would say I'm their hero and I'm godly. Not one. Both. Not a buddy without divine purpose nor a holy man without deep family bonds. And I told them that this was my goal. I wasn't pressuring them, just trying to help them become character-molding heroes one day. Your kids can too if you'll plant three seeds in them.

139

Seeds of character molding

The first seed of character molding is letting your kids know your character. As noted earlier, for Caleb to be open to the character I wanted to instill in him, he needed me to be vulnerable. He wanted to know the real me, warts and all. Although that's not how I was raised, I now try to be vulnerable for one reason: I love my son more than I love my privacy. I learned that kids open up when we share our story, warts and all.

A friend asked me, "What if you'd never known that Caleb wanted vulnerability?" I replied, "I still wouldn't know how to bond with him." My son and I had a friendship, but now we have a bond. It's a reminder of Dr. Bengtson's research – that faith legacies continue most when kids bond emotionally with parents, especially their fathers.

The second seed of character molding germinates when parents freely give respect, while earning their kids' respect. Living the motto, "give mine, earn yours" gives kids the security that I'll give my respect no matter what, while trying to earn yours. If this sounds one-sided, it is. Welcome to parenting. It's not fair, but it's what kids need. "Give mine, earn yours" opens kids' hearts to character worth copying.

Many parents talk down to kids, yet wonder why kids are disrespectful. Kids shouldn't have to navigate the choppy waters of youth while reconciling the hypocrisy of the opposite all-too-common reality: "give yours, earn mine." That's where I demand that you give me your respect, while expecting you to earn mine. Clichés like "because I said so" and "don't you dare question me" may sound fine as a parent, but they're debilitating for kids. When I started giving and earning respect, I didn't announce it. I just did it. And it changed everything.

The third seed sprouts when we become students of our kids' giftedness and dreams. In *Spiritual Parenting*, Michelle Anthony says, "We enlist ourselves as students of our children . . . to learn

about them specifically as the children God has entrusted to us."
Tedd Tripp goes further in *Shepherding a Child's Heart*:

> Most parents cannot quickly generate a list of strengths
> and weaknesses of their children. (They) have not sat
> down and discussed their short-term and long-term goals
> for their children. They have not developed strategies for
> parenting.

Even if you're not a student of your kids' character, they're students of yours. They're always listening. Always watching. They may say nothing now, but they're secretly hoping you'll dream big and back it up. Sure, declaring a big dream is risky, but aiming low is even riskier. Thankfully, kids tend to forgive over time, but what they don't forgive, especially decades later, are two character blockers: 1) a pattern of hypocrisy and 2) a failure to try.

Character blockers
Kids have a knack for spotting baloney. Nothing kills godly legacies faster than a pattern of hypocrisy. Kids don't expect perfection, but they reject your continually saying one thing and doing another. They're typically even fine with occasional lapses when accompanied by sincere apologies. Since a pattern of hypocrisy is obvious, though, it's often less dangerous than the stealthy second character blocker – not trying.

No thirteen-year-old says, "Mom, I'm so mad at you for not trying to mold my character." But twenty years later, they see better who you were as a parent. Good intentions aren't enough. Kids need to see you navigate stormy days so that they can learn to navigate theirs. They desperately want you to care enough to try, even if you struggle.

Character molding puts skin on a family vision by living what you love and loving what you live. It's fueled by integrity, not intentions. Examples, not excuses. Life stories, not life lectures.

It's simmered, not microwaved. Like great sauces, character needs heat, but not too much. Attentive simmering flavors kids without letting them boil over, melding all the flavors of your family character into your family's own "secret sauce."

Your family's secret sauce
Every family has a secret sauce of unique ingredients and recipes that define them. Ingredients are your chosen character qualities. Recipes are how you meld those qualities. No two families have the same secret sauce, because each family is unique. Can you articulate the character that defines you? If not, how could your kids pass down a legacy they can't explain?

Ironically, I learned this lesson while working at CiCi's. Before joining the CiCi's family, I didn't know how they made their sauce. I just knew that I craved it. Even better than their sauce, though, was their service. How did they become the Chick-fil-A of pizza with such intentional, friendly employees? Service was clearly a secret to their success. It made me want to join such an inspiring culture. My conclusion after serving fourteen years at this industry leader is one basic truth, which applies at both work and home:

It's all about the sauce and how you serve it.

What's your family's secret sauce and how well are you serving it? Are you creating a culture that kids crave? Are you letting it simmer, or are you applying too much heat to your kids?

Sauces aren't intended to be the entrée. They flavor everything else. So too, the goal isn't for kids to mimic your character; it's for godly character to flavor everything in them. It's enhancing their character with dabs of yours, not putting too much "sauce" on their plate. Three tools to flavor your family with an aromatic secret sauce are: 1) character ingredients, 2) character recipes, and 3) character letters.

Character ingredients

Great family character, like a great sauce, uses great ingredients. In addition to great ingredients, the key is ensuring your ingredients aren't a secret. To truly know your family's character, you need to articulate it in fun, memorable ways. A great place to start is the Secret Sauce exercise. You pick 26 A-to-Z character qualities that you want to define your family. It's a character version of Joshua 24:15: Choose for yourselves today your character qualities, but as for me and my house, we will emulate the Lord. This exercise can be done in many ways, but here's how I led my family to create its own secret sauce of character.

Before a family vacation, I gave them a long list of A-to-Z character qualities and asked each couple to jointly choose 26 character qualities – one for each alphabet letter – that would define their future family. On vacation, we shared our A-to-Z "ingredients" and why we chose them.

We laughed at how each couple's list reflected them. Josh and Robyn's list signified their nature (Quirky), love for animals (Zoo), and sensitive hearts (Grace). Leslie and Ryan used words like Present, Overflowing, and Yoked, reflecting their passion for abiding relationships. Caleb and Emily chose qualities like Grateful, Vulnerable, and Yielding, revealing their desperation for God. Each list reflected each couple's unique character.

What would your family members choose if they picked 26 A-to-Z character qualities? Would any word be picked by everyone? Only two words were chosen by everyone in our family – authentic and integrity. But if I could pick two ingredients to bake into a legacy, I'd probably pick authentic and integrity.

Seeing my kids choose their character qualities was one of the highlights of my life. I also loved how Ryan said, "Leslie and I picked words that describe who we want our family to be, even if we aren't that yet." Attaboy, Ryan! Whether he ended up with ten kids or none, Ryan was choosing upfront how to raise them. And, by the way, Ryan and Leslie surprised us that night by announcing they were pregnant with our first grandchild!

No, I can't promise grandchildren from this exercise, but I can promise a fresh glimpse into your family's future. You'll be enlightened and motivated to live your own character qualities with integrity and to help your kids do the same. Like Ryan and Leslie, you'll see that you aren't yet who you want to be, but you're choosing who you'll become. For illustrative purposes, here's how Anna and I visualized our A-to-Z character qualities.

Alba Family "Secret Sauce"

Authentic *Beliefs* CHOICES

Devoted

Encourager *Family*

Generous Humor **Integrity**

Jesus-follower KIND

Legacy-maker

Memories **NEVERTHELESS**

Obedient

Purposeful RELATIONAL

Quality

Transforming

SERVANT–
LEADER UNENTITLED

Visionary

WELL-DONE! *Xtraordinary*

Young-hearted Zealous

This exercise is powerful, personal, and fun. Nothing fancy. Try it using the Workbook exercise at www.timalba.com and watch it start shaping your family's character. It's also a great conversation starter. By displaying it at work, I've had many inspiring conversations with people who had not yet considered their family's character but now want to do so.

This exercise can serve as priming a pump of character. Once primed, it keeps gushing for years. Even preschoolers can grasp age-appropriate character lessons that flow into poignant applications, especially when you – their character hero – celebrate the character already within them. What hero has primed your character? Chances are, they used great ingredients to create the second part of a secret sauce – character recipes.

Character recipes
Unlike my mom's enchiladas that her friends couldn't replicate (because she didn't write down the recipe), you can pass down your character with "character recipes" – the stories behind your A-to-Z character qualities. I wrote one recipe per week for 26 weeks because I wanted my kids to understand my character qualities – the stories behind my life story. Kids love learning how you've become who you are, especially problems you've overcome. For example, here's our recipe for G – Generous:

> If you ask my kids who is the most giving, humble man they know, they'll say Grandpa Alba – my dad. It was frustrating sometimes as a kid seeing him give away so much time and money. But now I realize how I'm the beneficiary of Dad's outrageous generosity.
>
> Turns out, my parents were simply living out 2 Corinthians 9:6-7: "he who sows sparingly will also reap sparingly, and he who sows bountifully will also reap bountifully. Each one must do just as he has purposed in his heart, not grudgingly or under compulsion, for God loves a cheerful giver." Mom and Dad are predisposed

and ready to act. They aren't wealthy, but they're rich in generosity – the overflow of character.

I've joked that humble generosity skips a generation, so my kids have a chance. In reality, we taught them that generosity flows from hearts, not habits. When hearts overflow, so does giving. For example, I remember riding with Dad to someone's house to secretly give them cash. The amount didn't solve their financial woes, but Dad had it, so he gave it, expecting nothing in return. Over and over, I saw time and money flow without hesitation.

Generosity is contagious. It attracts and connects. While little kids love gifts, they later cherish the character those gifts reflect. Generosity also reflects the size of your world. When you live in a small world, you complain about small problems. But when you live in a big world, you see big possibilities, you dream big, and you live generously. You overflow.

Overflowing generosity originates from God, who gives to all generously and without reproach (James 1:5). Our cup overflows because God prepares a table for us and anoints our head with oil (Psalm 23:5). Jesus came to give overflowing life (John 10:10). And we overflow in hope by the Holy Spirit's power (Romans 15:13).

Generous kids are birthed from generous parents who overflow in love (1 Thessalonians 3:12). They speak from overflowing hearts (Luke 6:45). And they honor God from overflowing produce and first fruits (Proverbs 3:9, Deuteronomy 26).

I want to lead my kids to be unselfish and unsparing. Like their grandparents, they can have lavish love, sympathetic spirits, profuse praise, compassionate charity, and abundant actions. We may be conservative in doctrine, but we want to be liberal in giving.

Thankfully, God's generosity never skips a generation. We can all be conduits of God's overflowing grace because we're all beneficiaries of His overflowing generosity. Indeed, we're never more like God than when we cheerfully model His generosity.

My favorite story about character qualities, though, comes from the birth to our first grandchild, Cade Bolder Medlin. Months after he was born, I thought back and remembered one of the words Leslie had chosen for her A-to-Z character qualities seven months earlier – her B word was "Bold." I still get chills telling people how Cade the Bold, as we call him, is living proof that character qualities come alive when they become personal.

Your proof likely won't call you Grandma or Grandpa like Cade the Bold does, but it will help define your family's future when your ingredients mesh into flavorful family recipes. Still, kids need something more. They also need parents to personalize those qualities and recipes using the third part of secret sauces – character letters.

Character letters

All kids have character within them, but not every child has someone to reveal it. Kids need you to brag about their incredible qualities, not just complain about the bad ones. But how often do you brag on their character? Sadly, I tended to correct vices, not celebrate victories.

What would happen if, for every word of correction at them, you spoke two words of character into them? You'd define a legacy they want for themselves. Speaking character gives kids confidence of who they are in Christ. If you don't, the world will tell them who they are. Either way, someone will shape their character. Why not you? Why not the truth?

If you don't tell them, how will they know? Yes, you say you love them and are proud of them. You likely build their character. But do you tell them why you admire the character *already there*? I hadn't. But when my kids graduated high school, I wrote them a letter about why I admired their character. They loved their letters, but Caleb did something I never expected. He wrote back:

147

Dear Dad,

The older I get, the more I appreciate all you do. You are a man of God who puts his family above everything else. You came from a home where you were told what to do, and rarely given the why for doing it. Thank you for helping me understand why you do what you do.

The small things often have the greatest impact. I used to wonder what possible meaning could come of signing our names on a piece of paper and framing it above the stairs. I used to wonder of the purpose of so many paintings. Now I know.

You always think long term. We may not understand the purposes of things you do or ask us to do, but they are for our wellbeing. I stand in awe of all the seeds you planted in my life that have formed me into who I am.

With crosses, paintings, documents, scriptures, discipline, and occasional outbursts of wisdom, you made sure I knew what was important to you and why. You created an environment that points towards what you love and pursue – your Heavenly Father.

Dad, you are a man of respect, integrity, character, discipline, perseverance, success, and determination. But these characteristics don't define who you are. The Bible says we can't know God if we don't know love. What defines you is your love for the Lord.

You speak so often of legacy and the impact you want to leave. Your legacy won't be success as a CFO or father who provided for his kids, though those aren't bad things. It will be how you loved and pursued the Lord, and how you bettered His kingdom.

Out of love for the Lord, you've provided all that you have for your family. Out of love for the Lord, you have written a book, bestowing upon your family the blessings and knowledge bestowed upon you. In loving the Lord, your life has been revealed with the utmost clarity. The purpose and passion you live by, day after day, allow you to be faithful with what you have been given.

I am so proud to call you my dad and brother in Christ. I look up to you in so many ways. I admire your selfless service, as you kill yourself at work because the Lord calls you to give your best in all you do, settling for nothing less.

I admire how you love and seek Mom. I never doubted your love for her. You made sure we knew it too, something most kids never get to see. You would come home, flowers in hand, surprising Mom as she bursts into a huge smile. It was a blessing having that consistency and example in my life.

Thank you for all you do. I surely don't say it enough. I love you, Dad. Thank you for loving the Lord.

Caleb hadn't read this book, but his letter was like a mini version of it. Then again, your kids don't have to read your book to read you. What would happen if you exchanged letters with your kids about why you admire each other? What would you say? How might they respond? Your kids' letters would be unique, but the family resemblance would surely be remarkable because you share many character qualities.

The best part of Caleb's letter was that he wasn't just appreciating my character; he was choosing his own. My dream for him was now his own. His letter wouldn't have happened, though, if Anna and I hadn't become students of his character and showed him how to express it.

Expressing, modeling, and molding your kids' character in Christ – their Christ-esteem – puts them on the path to faithfulness. And nothing helps them walk that path more than their believing that they have the character to do so. The goal of character heroes isn't having perfect character; it's becoming more like the ultimate superhero who does.

The ultimate superhero

You can be your family's hero, but only one person can be their ultimate superhero: Jesus Christ. By embracing the cross, Jesus embraced us. He didn't go weakly to the cross; He "was determined to go" (Luke 9:51). He suffered the passion of the Christ with God-honoring passion.

When Jesus hung on the cross and said in John 19:30, "It is finished," sin's finish line was crossed. The debt was paid. The race, won. Sin's debt, cancelled. His purpose, realized. His prophecy, fulfilled. His victory, secured. His love, proven. His joy, priceless. His resurrection, inevitable. His invitation, riveting. His relationships, complete. His legacy, well done!

Jesus stuck to His story so that we can stick to ours. He crossed His finish line, allowing us to cross our own. He instilled timeless character in others, as can we. We too can live with Jesus' character qualities, which helps our kids want to emulate Him, the one true superhero.

Compelling vision and timeless character are foundational. As we'll see next, though, kids also need the third bond of well-done parenting – a captivating culture that inspires them to pass it on.

Choices to practice:

1. Who are your heroes and what makes them heroic?

2. Have you ever had a pattern of hypocrisy? If so, how?

3. What are your two favorite character qualities and why?

CULTURE

(PASS IT ON)

"These words . . . shall be on your heart. You shall teach them diligently to your sons and shall talk of them when you sit in your house and when you walk by the way and when you lie down and when you rise up" (Deuteronomy 6:6-7).

"Hear, my son, your father's instruction and do not forsake your mother's teaching; indeed, they are a graceful wreath to your head and ornaments about your neck" (Proverbs 1:8-9).

Chapter 13

Unique Family Promises

February 15, 2014, is a day I'll never forget. That's the day I looked tearfully into the eyes of my beautiful baby girl, hugged her tight, prayed a blessing over her new life, and proudly started walking. Arm in arm. Step by step. Seemingly a lifetime away stood her prince charming whose bushy brown beard was covered with tears. He couldn't believe he was getting to marry my daughter. (I couldn't believe it either.)

With all the memorization skills and strength I could muster, I choked out the four words feared by every loving father: "Her mother and I." Despite my denial-induced stupor, I found my assigned seat and witnessed something far greater than a beautiful wedding – the most worshipful experience of my life.

Overwhelmed, I put my arm around Anna, leaned in close, and whispered, "Wow. We raised her." I wasn't bragging. I was awed at what our little girl had grown to treasure. She planned her wedding so that her unchurched friends could experience real worship. She filled her wedding with the same two treasures that we had instilled in her – faith and family.

While I'd like to take credit for Leslie, I can't. She's the product of a culture forged by multiple generations of faithfulness. Still, I wondered if there had been a defining moment where it started for her. Indeed, there was, 26 years earlier at her baby dedication. That's the day I promised to raise her unto God . . . my first promise to Leslie of what she could expect from me, and my first promise to God of who would pass down a faithful legacy to Leslie: "Her mother and I."

Culture didn't force Leslie to become the inspiring woman she is. Culture enabled it. Leslie and her brothers had the benefit of something Anna and I also received from our parents – an expectation that faithfulness is the norm. My kids had to choose their own values, but culture positioned them to know how to choose well, want to, and, in turn, pass it down to their own kids.

Captivating culture – a culture that multiplies values through an inspiring environment of faithfulness – doesn't cram values down your throat. It cultivates a hunger and thirst for values. It nurtures and grooms. It invites kids to the party. Ever so slowly, kids grow to want godly values, albeit with their own unique flair. Our kids didn't copy our values; they created their own version of what they'd experienced.

Captivating family cultures share five elements. The first element – compelling vision – was applied in Chapter 6 with vision monuments. Chapter 12 introduced character heroes who flavor families with an aromatic secret sauce of the second element – timeless character.

The final three elements of captivating family cultures are explored in the next three chapters: unique family promises, memory tattoos, and heavenly hugs. These five elements create well-done legacies by bonding with your kids' hearts, funneling their beliefs, and shaping their dreams.

Made and kept promises

Well-done legacies start by deciding what your kids can expect from you – the promises you make and keep. What values do your kids expect from you? Have you ever told them? Chances are, you haven't yet clearly articulated your values and made them your vow to your kids. But you can.

Kids deserve more than "I did my best" excuses because we didn't know what to promise. And while kids love to point out our mistakes, they'd rather we mess up and fess up than float along with rudderless parenting. They want worthy promises to believe in and aspire to.

When we declare values that we promise to keep, we give kids a map and fuel. We aren't telling them exactly where to go. We're not hoping they'll figure it out. We're providing winning directions to worthy destinations. We're articulating and sharing values with which they deeply connect.

Making promises is a start, but keeping them does something miraculous in kids. It creates openness. For kids to believe in your values, they need to believe in you. A culture that makes and keeps worthy promises instills the ability for kids to trust you and trust God.

A promise is a claim of what someone can expect from you. But do your promises captivate your kids' hearts? They can if you'll make and keep unique family promises (UFPs). A UFP isn't just a claim. It's an aim. It points kids toward values they can own. It's part of their home training, as my dad called it – a unique home culture that I heard all the time and could count on every time. Dad didn't call them UFPs, but they were unique to us, drilled in us, and modeled for us. UFPs share three traits.

First, a UFP casts vision that *captures* your family's imagination. It's a promise shared by your family, yet it also uniquely stirs each child's heart. Many people can influence your kids, but no one else was appointed by God to know and win their hearts. Only you can lay a foundation of credible UFPs that they'll talk about and emulate decades later with their own kids.

Second, a UFP molds character that *seals* your family's imagination. Like a letter sealed with wax and a unique insignia, UFPs adhere to your kids' hearts. And even if they try in their youth to break your seal, they're prepared to one day make promises that their own kids can count on.

Last, a UFP crafts a culture that *multiplies* your family's imagination. Kids learn to extend your values about God when

155

your home is an offering unto God. Family values multiply when parents not only value their kids, but also make their kids a vow unto God. That's the secret of a virtuous woman in Proverbs 31:2 – her kids are her vow to God. She lives out this vow in literally every area of her life. One of the most impactful promises to give kids is a Proverbs 31 culture with the freedom to tweak those values with their own personal twist.

In *The Power of Why*, Richard Weylman describes a similar principle of transforming businesses by creating a unique value promise that asks, understands, and meets customers' needs. Weylman says,

> When your organizational culture is aligned with your promise, it makes your promise a reality. It determines how you run your business (and) mandates the support you give to customers and your team… The challenge is changing or improving (your culture) so that it can deliver your newfound Unique Value Promise.

Weylman's promises serve customers to advance sales; UFPs serve families to advance God's kingdom. Our goal isn't sales; it's souls. UFPs captivate families with memorable, creative applications. They're promises to God of what you'll instill in your family and promises to families of what God will instill in them. UFPs won't win popularity contests, but they'll win your kids' hearts and minds. Looking back, I can see where my first family promise originated – at the ultimate interview.

The ultimate interview

It was 3 p.m. on a Saturday in April. Twenty years old and brimming with confidence, I had made my best sales pitch a week earlier and returned to hear the master interviewer's answer. Gracious and firm, he slowly reached into his leather briefcase and pulled out a Big Chief tablet.

If you're too young to remember Big Chief tablets, they were note pads with a big chief on the cover. The irony was not lost. He was the big chief. I was the little warrior. With five full pages of questions, the master interviewer expected thoughtful answers to each probing question.

One hour of the interview passed. Two hours. After three hours, the ladies outside insisted we stop for dinner. Finally, it was over, right? Nope. After dinner, we retreated for another two hours. If nothing else, he thoroughly explored every area of my life in those five hours.

Without question, that was my most successful interview for one reason. It wasn't because of the eloquence of my vision; it was my elation at his verdict. The master interviewer wasn't an employer. He was Royce, my girlfriend's father, who agreed to let me to marry his "little lamb."

In reality, Royce didn't need five hours of Q&A because he already knew me . . . except when he asked, "What attracts you to my daughter?" (I was proud of what I didn't say!) Still, I think Royce's inquisition was to ensure I'd make and keep two promises: 1) that I would love his little lamb more than I love myself, and 2) that faith and family would matter most to me.

Decades later, life is so different. Kids grew, love deepened, and Alzheimer's took its toll. Still, those two promises remain. First, my vow to love Anna still stands: "I do." Second, the faith and family that mattered most back then are what still matter most now. They look different because they're no longer just Royce's story. They're Anna's and my story.

Are you preparing your family for the Master Interviewer? Are you making it easy for them to embrace their own saving faith so that they can kneel before the gracious, yet firm, Lamb of God and give an account of their faithfulness (1 Corinthians 3:10-15)?

No matter how it works exactly, know this: what will matter most to God then is what matters most to you now. His response, as well as your elation or despair, depends on if you love the Lamb of God more than you love yourself. The culture you lift up to your family now can be a crown you lay down at His feet in heaven.

I often wonder about our heavenly interview. Does God sit on His mercy seat or run to welcome us? Will He cry or will the only tears be ours of joy? Are we speechless or shouting praise? We can only imagine. But we don't have to imagine God's response to His faithful adopted family members: "Well done, good and faithful servant! . . . Enter into the joy of your Master" (Matthew 25:21). Three decades after my interview with Royce, I caught a glimpse of Royce's interview with God.

After fourteen grueling years of Alzheimer's, Royce's body was shutting down. Knowing he would soon pass, I leaned over and whispered my last promise to him, "Don't worry. I'll take good care of your girls." Then he took one last gasp and was gone. It was so peaceful.

Instantly, the last part of Matthew 25:21 became vividly real like never before. Yes, Royce surely enjoyed that verse's first promise – hearing God say, "Well done, good and faithful servant." But I watched Royce experience the ending promise – "Enter into the joy of your Master."

What will God say at your heavenly interview? Will you enter into His joy? Will your promises be crowns you lay at His feet? Or will you wish you had made and kept promises that honor Him?

What you may need to do as your kids grow, though, may be the hardest part – let go. Letting go isn't giving up. It's releasing kids to fly on their own. It's trusting God's grace and your preparation. It's determining to be faithful, not letting your faithfulness be determined by theirs.

Thankfully, as we've seen, most kids who bond with godly parents will carry on a godly legacy. But exceptions happen. Our mission is to prepare kids to be exceptional, not the exception – kids who are the signature of well-done parenting. Dianna Booher says it in her exceptional book, *Your Signature Work*, "God will be the final appraiser of the value we create."

We prepare kids to choose well, but *they* choose. Too many parents languish in poor choices made by prodigal kids who are the exception, not the rule. Yes, parenting seems impossible at times, but we don't have to be victims of our kids' choices. We can promise to accept a Mission Him-possible – a seemingly impossible mission of raising kids unto Him.

Mission Him-possible

"Your mission, should you decide to accept it, is to …"

Mr. Phelps accepted the challenge of seemingly impossible missions in the television show *Mission Impossible*. He led a team to fulfill missions bigger than themselves. His challenges, like our family dreams, become reality when effective plans are embraced, despite all odds.

Families are also challenged to overcome obstacles and fulfill missions bigger than themselves. Mr. Phelps fulfilled his missions in a few days; ours take a lifetime. Mr. Phelps directed his team's efforts, but God directs our steps (Proverbs 16:9). Our missions differ because our whys differ. While Mr. Phelps' missions *seemed* impossible, ours actually *are* impossible without God. With God, however, they're promises – vows – we make to our family to raise them unto Him.

Him-possible missions expose a God bigger than your imagination, who gives dreams bigger than you can imagine. Anything less is inconsistent with His nature. God is too significant to give you an insignificant mission. Your family's mission is as big as your family's God. Big God, big mission. Little god, little mission. It's also as big as your promises. Many people love the lovable. But Aspirers also love people like Ellen who've reached the end of their rope.

Ellen and Ashley looked like many grandmothers and teenage moms who attend our preschool ministry. As Ellen cuddled Ashley's precious newborn girl, though, Ellen shared a shocking story, not about Ashley's youth, but about her family tree.

As an unwed fifteen-year-old herself, Ellen gave birth to Ashley's mom, who bore Ashley at the same tender age of fifteen. Now, fifteen years later, Ashley was the third generation of fifteen-year-old unwed moms, making Ellen a great grandmother at age forty-five.

As a forty-five-year-old at the time too, I couldn't imagine being a great grandparent. I wasn't judging. I was asking myself how different this little newborn's life could be one day if her family could make and keep a promise to change their family tree. And I asked myself: What promises do I need to make so that my family won't repeat my mistakes?

We don't have to be branches of dysfunctional family trees. We can graft in faithfulness by pruning out the branches of victims, regret, and busy-ness. In Steve Farrar's book *Point Man*, he asks if negative families are consigned to being links in negative family chains. His conclusion:

> Absolutely not! The good news is you can forge a new link in the chain. You can make a difference. You can make a conscious decision to become a rock and role model who will change your generational chain from a negative to a positive. The choices you make today will not only affect your children, but their children, and their children, and their children. One man can make a difference . . . one man who chooses to be a rock.

Kids love to know that we overcame a negative past, but they also need to see us live a praiseworthy present and consistently live what we preach about godly living. Just ask Solomon.

Although Solomon was famously wise, his sons failed. But Solomon wasn't the first Jewish king to miss the mark as a dad. Solomon and his brothers multiplied the polygamy, rape, and murder seen in their dad, David. David was king due to Saul's disobedience. Saul became king when God rejected Samuel's rebellious sons. And Samuel followed Eli because Eli's sons were so sinful. Unless your family is your vow, your godly legacy is one generation away from extinction.

Instead of creating disciples of you, craft *disciplers* who multiply faithfulness through others. Sadly, disciplers are rare. Type "discipler" into a word processor and it inserts a red squiggly line. It doesn't recognize the term. Kids may not recognize the term either, but they recognize the effort. And even if your kids don't yet embrace your culture, don't blame yourself. Parents prepare; children choose. Parents pray; children change. God knows if you're putting faithfulness on a tee so they can whack it.

Paul teed up Timothy, Titus, and Archippus by promising a fulfilling life in Christ and backing it up with a captivating culture of faithfulness. Paul told Timothy: "The things which you have heard from me in the presence of many witnesses, entrust these to faithful men, who will be able to teach others also" (2 Timothy 2:2). Paul told Titus to lead people "to meet pressing needs, so that they will not be unproductive" (Titus 3:14). And for Archippus: "Take heed to the ministry which you have received in the Lord that you may fulfill it" (Colossians 4:17).

Who's your Timothy, Titus, or Archippus? Mine were named Leslie, Joshua, and Caleb – my little budding disciplers who blossomed with their own UFP cultures. My kids needed vision and character, but they also need UFPs to become purposefully

161

courageous and passionately contagious. Vision monuments like a *Declaration of Him-dependence* in Chapter 6 are UFPs of compelling family vision. A-to-Z secret sauces in Chapter 12 are also UFPs to promise an aromatic family character. Here's another UFP example – parenting vows.

Parenting vows

We make wedding vows, promising to be a faithful wife or husband. So why not make parenting vows, promising to be a faithful mom or dad? Why not tell your family (and God) what they can expect from you? Unlike wedding vows spoken once and forgotten, parenting vows can be shared over and over in fresh, age-appropriate ways.

If you were to write parenting vows to your kids, what would you promise? Know this: if you'll promise it, kids will watch to see if you keep it. I wish I'd done this when my kids were little, but even as adults they want to know what I'll promise (because we never stop parenting, right?). You can write personal parenting vows or you might mirror traditional wedding vows with specific parenting promises such as:

> I, Dad, take you, Leslie Marie, to be my daughter, to have and hold, from this day forward. For better or worse, for richer or poorer, in sickness or health, till death do us part. According to God's Holy Scriptures, I pledge myself to you.

I wanted my parenting vow, though, to reflect our unique family culture. Therefore, on a special family vacation, I gave my kids parenting vows based on Anna's and my character qualities from Chapter 12. For example, here's my parenting vow to Leslie and her husband, Ryan:

I, Dad, take you, Leslie Marie Medlin and Ryan Keith Medlin, to be my daughter and son-in-law, to lead you as unto Christ. I promise to have and hold you, no matter how you respond. For better or worse, for richer or poorer, in sickness or health, I will love and cherish you till death do us part. According to God's Holy Scriptures, I will provide you with a home built upon these qualities:

- Authentic – the reality of character
- Beliefs – the foundation of character
- Choices – the proof of character
- Devoted – the depth of character
- Encourager – the celebration of character
- Family – the extension of character
- Generous – the overflow of character
- Humor – the light-heartedness of character
- Integrity – the credibility of character
- Jesus-follower – the source of character
- Kind – the caring of character
- Legacy-maker – the perpetuity of character
- Memories – the tattoos of character
- Nevertheless – the persistence of character
- Obedience – the position of character
- Purposeful – the rationale of character
- Quality – the standard of character
- Relational – the conduit of character
- Servant-leader – the duality of character
- Transforming – the metamorphosis of character
- Unentitled – the humility of character
- Visionary – the horizon of character
- Well-done! – the finality of character
- Xtraordinary – the effect of character
- Young-hearted – the youthfulness of character
- Zealous – the passion of character

This I vow, I promise, and I choose . . . to make it easy for you to be a faithful servant who one day hears God say, "Well done!"

Your vow might be short or it might be long like mine. The key isn't the length of your vow; it's the length you'll go to keep it.

Oh how I wish parenting came with do-over coupons to redeem with kids, but it doesn't. I can, though, redeem my kids and grandkids with a culture of kept promises and sincere apologies. For if there's one promise, I want Leslie to know I'll always keep, it's who will always be there for her: "Her mother and I."

What eternity-changing promises could you make for your kids? For heaven's sake, though, whatever you promise, keep it. In the next chapter, you'll see how to make those promises become vividly real – by instilling indelible memories they can't forget and wouldn't want to.

Choices to practice:

1. How would your kids describe your family's culture?

2. For what broken promises do you need to apologize?

3. What promises have you been making to your family?

Chapter 14

Memory Tattoos

Who's on your short list of champions that have invested in you? Some of mine are Don, Carol, Anna, Dean, Paul, Joe, and Jimmy. None of them have a body tattoo, but each of them seared something in me far more permanent – memory tattoos – indelible memories I can't forget and wouldn't want to.

Don (aka Dad) seared memories of humble generosity. From Carol, it was a mother's love. From Anna, unending devotion. From Dean Smith, relational mentoring. From Paul Kimball, sacrificial teaching. From Joe Croce, unrelenting excellence. And from Jimmy Draper, inspiring faith. Each of them created memory tattoos I can't remove or cover up because of one reason: they stirred my soul.

Whose life do you stir? Who carries your mark? What unforgettable memories of you stir your family's soul? Have you ever shared with them the memories you hope to create? Simon Peter did.

Simon Peter wrote, "I (want) to stir you up by way of reminder (and) be diligent that at any time after my departure you will be able to call these things to mind" (2 Peter 1:13, 15). How about you? Like Simon Peter, are you etching indelible, stirring memories?

If a picture is worth a thousand words, a culture is worth a thousand pictures. Kids need family cultures that string together captivating mental pictures and speak their language, grab their attention, and stir their hearts with priceless memories. Moment by moment, skeletons of godly legacies get skin in captivating cultures of authentic, everyday faithfulness.

For example, my dream of seeing Jesus embrace my kids is so vivid, it feels like a memory. I talk about it all the time. But I'm not trying to sell my dream. I'm trying to stir my kids to remember a family culture that helps them create their own dreams.

Kids don't magically wake up one day ready to pass down godly values. My wife, the master of teachable memories, teaches parents how it takes an intentional, everyday approach. Anna turned washing dishes with a toddler into Scripture-memorizing memories that Leslie still cherishes. Meals, shopping, band competitions, sporting events, and homework all became Anna's daily deposits that drew our kids' interest.

Memory tattoos occur spontaneously, but not randomly, in a culture that softens kids' soils. For example, my two-seat convertible became a top-down, music-cranking, arms-flapping way to prepare my daughter to receive love when words couldn't. But that's the beauty of memory tattoos. They're simple tools for a superior purpose.

Cultures change when behaviors change. Behaviors change when treasures change. Treasures change when people connect with fulfilling treasures that *they* choose. And that's what memory tattoos do. They help kids become receptive by changing what they choose.

Memory tattoos funnel beliefs, which fixes behavior. Many parents get it backwards – they focus on fixing kids' behaviors, which crumbles their kids' receptivity to funneling their beliefs.

Home should be a catalyst of celebration and a launching pad of legacies. Kids need a home field advantage that crafts champions. Paul wasn't a parent, yet he rekindled Timothy's flickering flame into a raging champion: "I am mindful of the sincere faith within you, which first dwelt in your grandmother Lois and your mother Eunice, and I am sure that it is in you as well. For this reason, I remind you to kindle afresh the gift of God which is in you ..." (2 Timothy 1:5-6).

You're kindling your kids' passions, right? Well, maybe. It depends on your home culture. Culture needs vision and character, but culture trumps vision and character because it proves if vision and character are real. Culture is a long-term investment made with countless little deposits. When we invest in kids, their choices improve. And when we're busy or distracted, kids get drained like an over-drafted checking account. Therefore, kids need daily deposits in their culture account.

Culture account

Kids have culture accounts that get opened with parents' deposits. Some deposits are small or draw little interest. Others never seem to show up. Still, we make deposits to keep kids positive and avoid negative life balances. Instead of getting upset at our kids' withdrawals, we need to build portfolios of values by investing consistently, tracking progress, and staying the course.

Culture accounts prove the power of compounding interest and consistent investing. For example, $1 invested at 1% compounding interest becomes $1.64 after fifty years. At 10% interest, it compounds to $65.11. But after fifty years of investing $1 *daily,* that $65.11 grows to $467,309.27.

What would your kids look like as fifty-year-olds if you deposited a memory tattoo in them daily? You're not stuffing humble-conviction in a mattress. You're making deposits that generate *their* interest and watching God compound it. Then track their progress and stay the course.

Cultures worth celebrating also need you to involve others in crafting it. That's how Joe Croce built a pizza empire and a service phenomenon at CiCi's Pizza. Every CiCi's employee – receptionist, VP, dishwasher, or truck driver – had to wow people. No one was exempt. And we all benefited. One day, Joe gave me 245,000 frequent flyer miles and said, "Take your family to Hawaii." Wow, what a deposit! What a tattoo! By engaging me in his culture, Joe engaged me in his mission. And so can you with your family.

By engaging kids in your culture, you're searing tattoos like Lois and Eunice, whose timid Timmy became a bold Timothy. They later received heavenly crowns, not for what Timothy did for God, but for investing in him and preparing him for a heavenly homecoming.

Lynda Bethea was going home when saying, "Don't hate these men. They need Jesus." The martyr Stephen prayed, "Lord, do not hold this sin against them!" (Acts 7:60). And Jesus said, "Father, forgive them; for they do not know what they are doing" (Luke 23:34). They all prayed for their killers and went home because they lived the same way, as did Grandpa Loyd.

Unconscious on his deathbed, Grandpa Loyd victoriously arose with arms outstretched, mouth gaping open, and eyes gazing toward heaven. Then he slumped back and died.

How could a nearly lifeless man rise miraculously and pass peacefully? It's because he was going home. He pointed to heaven in death because he had pointed his family to heaven in life. My mom is a testimony of his home culture, just as your kids are a testimony of yours.

Is your home culture helping your kids be receptive? Is it searing the indelible memory tattoos you hope to see in your kids, grandkids, and beyond? Here are four tools to create your own tattoos.

1. Family blogs
2. Family portraits
3. Selfless service
4. Hope nuggets

Family blogs

Many bloggers instruct and inspire followers, but struggle to get their families to follow their advice. Solomon was a dad who used his version of blogs – proverbs – to create tattoos of instruction and inspiration in his nation and his kids. Here's a tool to instruct and etch inspirational tattoos into your kids' memories called "family blogs" – the stories behind your life story.

My first family blogs told the stories behind my Fifty Pursuits (from Chapter 2). With one blog per week for fifty weeks, my kids learned a whole new side of me. They now know why Pursuit #7 "Anna's embrace" is much more than hugs, why Pursuit #35 "Hot showers" reflects success-shaping sacrifice when selling Bibles door-to-door, and why Pursuit #39 – "CiCi's Pizza" built a legacy, not just a career. Here's an example: Pursuit #8 "Loving Anna" – which I wrote on Valentine's Day.

Opposites attract, but they can also divide over time. Although Anna and I are complete opposites, our opposites shape our marriage and parenting. I'm focused; she's fun-loving. I'm persistent and purposeful; she's pleasant and patient. Through it all, though, my wife is still my girlfriend who makes it easy to love her:

- She expresses love in every moment – a loving mom
- She's a "China doll" without admitting it – a true beauty
- She complements & compliments – an integral partner
- She trusts & forgives – a support network
- She stands by me regardless – an undaunted advocate
- She submits without being lesser – a biblical role-model
- She serves God like it's a privilege – a faithful servant
- She loves other families' kids – a preschooler mentor
- She lets me think her ideas are mine – a prideless teammate
- She's the master of the simple recipe – a hunger buster

- Her heart skips a beat when I arrive – a timeless lover
- She's exactly what I need – a heavenly God-send

Men need respect even more than love, so the Bible tells wives to respect their husbands. Women need extra love, so men are told to love their wives. Thus, respect is Anna's gift to me, and love is my gift to her.

Loving Anna is not only a gift to my wife, it's also a gift to my kids. The best way to help my kids want to be faithful to a loving God is for them to see Dad being faithful to a loving Mom.

Anna enjoys big gifts, like her 20th anniversary ring. But it's the symbolic gifts that she loves most, like flowers for no reason or opening her door. And since she expects so little, I love exceeding her expectations.

Yes, Babe, love is a choice, and you make it easy on Valentine's Day and every day.

You could do this in five weeks using your Five Passions or in twenty weeks with your Twenty Pursuits. I also wrote blogs for my 26 A-to-Z character qualities as a gift to my kids.

Family blogs aren't fancy. You're just sharing your life stories so that your kids will choose their own. Family blogs help your kids become receptive to a godly legacy, as does the next memory-creating tool – family portraits.

Family portraits

Two of the best ways to increase kids' receptivity are praise and questions. When you praise them and ask their opinions, kids learn to reciprocate. You're not praising to get praised. You're creating tattoos of praise. If you pounced on positives, not mistakes, they'd be more receptive, right?

For example, I never thought my *Fifty Reasons It's a Privilege to Be Your Husband* list for Anna would result in a Father's Day gift from my kids called *Fifty Reasons You Are an Awesome Father* (Chapter 6). I enjoyed seeing the big events on their list, but I especially cherished the little daily deposits that stuck, such as: "loving your kids' mother well," "encouraging your kids to pursue their dreams," "making church a priority every week," and "laying a spiritual foundation in your kids' lives." Turns out, all these little deposits were winning their hearts.

The second part – asking kids' opinions – requires humility and vulnerability. Ironically, this clicked for me when seeing Forbes Anderson's home portraits of his lovely wife and daughters. I wondered if I could create a symbolic portrait of my family's character. The answer is the second memory-creating tool, "home portrait," uses both praise and questions by asking family members to describe each other in three words.

The scary thing is that kids will tell you if you ask. Still, I had to know, so I asked my kids who were 10, 13, and 16 years old to describe me in three words, which I kept in my planner as a goal to become a better dad. After six years, I asked again.

Another nine years later, I asked them to describe all family members in three words and send me a fun photo of themselves. Then my son and I created a Christmas gift of everyone's three words for each other. Anna's portrait (photo and words) is shown in the Workbook at www.timalba.com, but here are their three words to describe Anna:

Loving, Grace-filled, True	by Tim
Welcoming, Giving, Loving	by Ryan
Selfless, Thoughtful, Genuine	by Leslie
Fun!, Christmas!, Intercessor	by Josh
Parties, Babies, Gracious	by Robyn
Loving, Gentle, Selfless	by Caleb
Servant-hearted, Compassionate, Tender	by Emily

Something wonderful happens in this exercise. There's power in asking and power in praising one another. And seeing these words and photos sears memories you'll never forget. Some of my family cried. Some laughed. Others said they had no idea that others saw those qualities in them. When I reminded them of how they described me nine and fifteen years earlier, my son said, "Dad, it's amazing how you've changed. The first time, we said you're purposeful and tenacious. You're still those things, but now you're also a learner and generous." Wow, they saw something in me that I didn't see in myself – I was changing.

You can't change what you don't know. Therefore, ask them, and work on what they'll say in a year or five years from now. Then again, other than God's opinion, whose opinion matters more than your family's?

Selfless service

The third memory-creating tool was one of Anna's greatest gifts to our kids – a home cradled in selfless service. Our kids assumed every family served like that. They didn't know better. She started by having them pick up after themselves. Then they had to pick up after each other. Did they want to? No! They'd whine, "But, Mom, it's not mine." And that's where Anna's tattoos of selfless service kicked in, by consistently modeling and expecting it. After years of practice, they picked up after others without being told.

We can force kids when they're young, but will they keep serving later? Likely yes, if drawn into it. Our kids saw Mom cry with the hurting, pray for the needy, and love the unlovely. Each act of service was insignificant by itself, but Anna's countless little service tattoos crafted a selfless culture and seared memories of service that our kids now mirror as adults.

Kids need to see parents model it, but they also need to do it themselves. 6 Stones Mission Network – a coalition of churches, schools, local governments, and business leaders that selflessly serves needy families in its community – uses four steps to create a service culture: 1) I do, you watch. 2) I do, you help. 3) You do,

I help. 4) You do, I watch. 6 Stones' volunteers, like kids, can learn to give back blessings, not just receive them.

Selfless service isn't what you do after you're done with your day; it's how you live your day. It's not just a spiritual gift from God; it's your gift to bless God's people. It's how kids follow in your footsteps while walking their own path.

In addition to "Chore Charts," Anna teaches parents to take time when kids are attentive – at meals – to share one thing they did today to serve their siblings. Why? Because the last person kids want to serve is a sibling. You might use a "Serve Chart," give gold-star stickers or privileges, spend extra one-on-one time, or anything that turns selfish natures into selfless norms.

Selfless service cultures aren't passed down with gift cards and plaques. They're etched with repetition and expecting nothing in return. My parents showed me the joy of cleaning gutters for widows, taking special needs adults shopping, singing at nursing homes, and packing your car with another family so that they too can go to church. My parents selflessly served in silence, but their joy spoke volumes.

Selfless legacies aren't microwaved. They're simmered, like crock pots, through how we serve, not what we deserve. How could you create tattoos of selfless service that your kids will one day want too?

Hope nuggets
After investing, instructing, inspiring, praising, asking, and serving your family, there's one more memory-creating tool: hope nuggets of celebration. It's tough sometimes, though, to find attitudes or actions worthy of celebration. We may need to look really hard to find these hope nuggets. Like old-time gold miners, three actions unearth hope nuggets in the dog days of nugget-less parenting: dig, sift, and celebrate.

First, we dig. But we can't just dig out gold. The gold is buried deep under crusty surfaces. We have to learn where to look, because treasures worthy of celebration can be hard to extract.

Next, we sift. Treasures are found by tirelessly sifting through mounds and mounds of junk. We often want to give up, but we can't, for their sake and ours. Sifting isn't fun, but thankfully it leads to celebrations.

Finally, we celebrate our kids' nuggets of hope. When we do, kids find hope. We're not giving out participation trophies; we're unearthing treasures buried within them. We catch kids doing things right and etch celebration tattoos that bond us together when bad choices could tear us apart. Here's my favorite hope nugget – Leslie's poem *The Doorkeeper's Vision*.

The Doorkeeper's Vision

Jesus – here, your provision is sufficient
here, all my needs and desires are met in You.

your word is my bread, your love my garment
your spirit my delight & joy.

your wind is my freedom, your mercy my covering
your faithfulness my consistency, your truth my reality.

your mystery is my glory, your judgments my treasured jewels
your boundaries are my meadow in which to run.

your face is my strength, your grace my abundance
your depths my wisdom, your riches my inheritance.

your cup is my overflow, your paths my peace,
your plans my prosperity.

your right hand is my support, your gentleness my greatness
your hope my foundation, your friendship my intimate
communion.

your process is my adventure, your presence my pleasure
your river my wellspring, your redemption my rejoicing.

your will is my surrender, your call my yes
your love my eyes, your narrow way my delight.

your cross is my vow, your affection my sole satisfaction
your beauty my gaze, your courts the better place.

your race is my invitation, your baton my joy,
your prize my ONE goal.

so I run. through your fields of provision,
trusting who you are in this season.

the sky is turning blue, the ocean is growing wide.
in your presence, Jesus, dawn and dusk collide.

To truly appreciate Leslie's poem, though, you have to know Leslie. No one loved Jesus more than teenager Leslie, but she pushed boundaries. Then, years later, I saw an amazing nugget of hope. While strolling together along a quiet tree-lined path, I looked over and saw Leslie joyfully frolicking in a grassy meadow. As her head tilted back and her arms stretched toward heaven, I recalled my favorite line from her poem to God: "your boundaries are my meadow in which to run."

My little boundary-pusher had grown to emulate her mother – an inspiring woman running joyfully within God's boundaries. What a nugget! And what a question: Do your kids learn at home that God's boundaries are their meadow in which to run?

In *Boundaries for Leaders*, Dr. Henry Cloud says that we get what we create or allow. It's true at home and work alike. But we can't just allow godly legacies to happen. We must create them. For kids to want a godly legacy, we need to create tattoos of acceptance and celebration, not anxiety and correction.

Leslie's *poem* also illustrates another core parenting principle:

Kids grow to reflect
the culture they've grown to expect.

What do your kids expect from you? Based on your example, what will they celebrate as adults? Almost anything can craft celebration nuggets. Janelle McGee adds a Christmas ornament annually of a key memory from the year. Eric and Leslie Bartel created "Our Family Rules," a poster of six age-appropriate choices (words and pictures) for their preschoolers.

All these tools – family blogs, family portraits, selfless service, and hope nuggets – sear unforgettable memory tattoos into your kids' hearts if you'll learn what motivates them. For example, which of Gary Chapman's five love languages motivates your kids? Emphasize each child's love language, but use all of them to improve your kids' receptivity. Even if words of affirmation aren't their love language, who doesn't want to be affirmed? For quality time, have pizza-and-pursuits family nights to unpack your Fifty Pursuits. Give timeless gifts like my daughter's warrior fabric. Serve together on a family mission trip or at a ministry like 6 Stones or KiDs Beach Club®, an innovative after school program that's "Making Jesus Cool at School! ®". Become a serial hugger, even if physical touch isn't your deal. For when you're a student of your kids, you're preparing them to become a teacher.

The student becomes the teacher
Have you had mentors who pour themselves into you? Beyond my parents, Dr. Nathan Jones was both an encourager and a challenger. Nathan knew my qualities and my faults, yet he saw something in me that others didn't and he was determined to stir it up.

Many years later came Nathan's priceless memory tattoo. While eating together at our favorite burger joint, I shared a life lesson that I had applied at work and home. Nathan dropped his fork, slowly tilted back his chair, nodded in subtle approval, and proudly proclaimed, "The student has become the teacher." He felt that his years of investments had compounded with interest.

Dear mom or dad, let me encourage you . . . never give up on the dream of seeing your student become the teacher. Kids need instruction, but instruction isn't enough. They also need a champion to create memories that stir their souls and draw their interest. And no matter how you feel right now, you can do this. When you do, you'll likely one day experience the greatest of all embraces, as described in the next chapter – Heavenly Hugs.

Choices to practice:

1. What memory tattoos have you etched into your family?

2. What three words would your kids use to describe you?

3. What kind of home culture do you want your family to expect?

Chapter 15

Heavenly Hugs

A week before my seventeenth birthday, I was daydreaming about my girlfriend and two-a-day football practices. One was lovely; the other, not so much. Little did I know I would soon face the crippling consequences of a default choice . . . three seconds of terror that transformed me, as well as my kids born a decade later.

As I stacked hay bales on a conveyor, a spinning tractor shaft snagged my jeans leg, twisted it into a knot, and started pulling me in. Instinctively, I yanked back as hard as I could from the tractor that was pulling me toward death or a crippled, mangled future. Then it happened. Somehow my jeans started ripping. Up my left leg. Across my waist. Down my right leg. I looked down and my jeans were gone. All that remained were bare legs, undershorts, and a belt holding nothing but tiny jeans fragments.

Dazed and trembling, I couldn't move. It was as if I'd been watching from above, powerless to change my fate. No one was around to see it happen, turn off the tractor, or pull my body from the wreckage. Only God could have miraculously ripped away those jeans. After coming to myself, all I could do was stare blankly at the machinery that chugged along with a dull hum as if nothing happened.

I never meant to dangle my jeans over a tractor shaft. It just happened. So too, we don't intentionally dangle our kids over danger. Still, it happens, causing parents to feel stripped down to their emotional nakedness, asking, "How in the world did my kids get snagged by my default choices?"

But you don't have to live a dangerous, dull life that keeps chugging along. You can live with an exclamation point now and hear God's exclamation point in heaven. You can enjoy God's embrace before entering heaven by living victoriously before your kids, not vicariously through them. You can give them a captivating culture that prepares them to receive the greatest of all embraces – the two kinds of heavenly hugs.

"Well-done!" hug

First is the "well done!" heavenly hug – the intimate, one-on-one embrace between Jesus and you. You'll lay your crowns at His feet, hear Him say, "Well done!" and enter into His joy. It's the homecoming reserved for anyone found faithful.

In order to visualize that moment for my family, I asked Keith Lewis to paint a man kneeling before Jesus and burying his head in Jesus' chest. Jesus' nail-scarred hands welcome him with an I've-been-waiting-for-you-so-long embrace. I told Keith that I had only one requirement: the man had to be like me – bald. Keith, though, didn't paint some bald guy with Jesus. He painted *me* with Jesus. Just the two of us, in an intimate "well done!" hug.

Now imagine *you* in that scene. Just Jesus and you. Embracing. Resting. Celebrating. You're oblivious to the angels giving praise, the streets of gold reflecting His glory, and His radiating light warming your resurrected skin. All you see is a nail-scarred, forgiving Savior who couldn't wait to see you face to face.

Even better, imagine Him doing the same with *your kids*.

Still, as unimaginable as this hug will be, another hug awaits.

"Welcome home!" hug

The second heavenly hug is the "welcome home!" hug with everyone who helped you enjoy a heavenly homecoming. Imagine all the people lining up for that group hug. I'll hug the Apostle Paul for his undaunted devotion, Susanna Wesley for being a faithful mom, and Paul Kimball for sacrificing his dreams. I'll hug my parents and sisters for a godly heritage, Nathan Jones for sharpening my iron, and my wife and kids for a joyful journey.

I'll hug those "strange" Americans who, nearly 100 years ago, never knew the future generations that would be transformed by their sacrificial love for a young Mexican mother. I'll hug Grandpa Loyd, Lynda Bethea, Ryan Christian, relatives, teachers, co-workers, and friends who passed down their faithful legacy to me and embraced their hope in Jesus so that I can embrace mine.

And I wonder, who in heaven can't wait to hug me?

How about you? Who in heaven do you want to hug? And who's already there that can't wait to hug *you*?

Where to start

Heavenly hugs are the fruit of compelling vision, timeless character, and captivating cultures. To enjoy that fruit, though, you must start. Right where you are, not when you think your family is ready. Do your best and apply the lesson learned at a peanut farm by John Meador.

John's dad decided his teenager needed a "real job." So he dropped off John in a peanut field. No training, no experience, and no clue where to start. John just knew that his job was to hoe weeds. His 400-pound mountain of a boss barely glanced at John and barked, "Grab a hoe. Pick a row. It's that simple."

We've all entered thorny situations with no plan and no confidence. So we do the only thing we can do. We pick a row and start hoeing. That's what Anna and I did as new parents when God dropped us off hundreds of miles from home at a new job. With no family, no friends, and no training as parents, we did our best and learned along the way. But you're better prepared. You now have a hoe (a dream and a plan) and a row (family and adopted family). It's time to grab your "hoe" and get after it.

As a young parent, I wanted to do better, but I tended to be a default parent who raised kids how I was raised, not how they needed me to be. I unknowingly dangled them over danger by being busy, distracted, and familiar. It took writing this book to realize that living my dreams isn't enough. I had to communicate and connect with my kids. Then one day, out of left field, teenager Caleb texted me:

> I know you started writing your book to share your "why" with Leslie, Joshua, and me. But just so you know, through the process of writing it, you learned how to communicate to us the things you wrote about. You grew as your book grew. I'm proud of you, Dad.

Caleb didn't understand family cultures. He just wanted more of what I had started doing. A captivating family culture may not be cool, but even teenagers know it when they see it and hear it. And they long for it, even if they can't explain it.

Can your family explain your home culture? Are you pursuing them well and communicating along the way? That's the beauty of captivating home cultures – they prepare kids to receive God's embrace and prevent them from being dangled over danger.

Choices to practice:
1. What default consequences have you had to live with?

2. How do you imagine your heavenly hug with Jesus?

3. Who will want to hug you in heaven?

The Result of Real Hope

Hope as a parent isn't based on your kids' choices. Hope comes from doing your part and trusting God to do His. You instill the vision, character, and culture that make it easy for kids to know *how* to be faithful and *want* to. God's part is drawing them into an intimate relationship with Himself.

Paul told his spiritual child, Timothy, how to lead his own spiritual children: "storing up for themselves the treasures of a good foundation for the future, so that they may take hold of that which is life indeed" (1 Timothy 6:19). That's the result of real hope – treasures in heaven and life indeed on earth.

You prepare kids to pursue heavenly treasures by pursuing the real life in Christ found right here. Every Christian parent wants that legacy. It can be your family's legacy too. But even if your kids reject your faith, God won't reject you. If you'll proudly present God to your family now, God will proudly present you to His family in heaven.

You're preparing and praying for your kids, not choosing for them or forcing change on them. You're bonding with their hearts, funneling beliefs, and shaping dreams. You're putting faithfulness on a tee so they can whack it and putting them on the path to faithfulness so they can walk it.

> You're making it *your* mission
> to make it *their* mission
> to hear God say, "Well done!"

Therefore, you'll never be the same . . . and neither will your kids. You're more than well intended. You've done well.

Well done, Mom and Dad!

Your Next Steps

In order to download a **free companion Workbook** and get more resources to apply this book's legacy-making lessons with your family or small group, visit **www.TimAlba.com** and **www.WellDoneMomAndDad.com**.

Get Tim's bi-weekly blog mailed to your inbox by signing up at **www.TimAlba.com/blog**. You'll receive ongoing inspirational content to put your family on the path to faithfulness. Topics include parenting, home/career leadership, character, faith, and family.

To have Tim speak at an event or to simply discuss a matter, please contact him at:

TimAlbaWD@gmail.com
www.TimAlba.com

About the Author

As a husband/dad, CFO, and executive pastor, Tim Alba has a unique ability to share inspiring success principles learned at both home and work. This book is the culmination of a lifelong pursuit of his passion: to hear God say, "Well done!" and help others do the same.

Tim's story is one of simple obedience. When God called Tim to leave his dream job as CFO and part-owner of CiCi's Pizza to serve his church full-time, he joyfully obeyed. Eight years later, when God led him to step aside from his pastoral role and serve as a volunteer advisor to his church, Tim again saw God turn simple obedience into a whole new world of blessings.

Tim's family leadership was featured in *Stories of True Financial Freedom: God's Impact in Real Lives* by Crown Financial Ministries. And his work leadership was featured in *Your Signature Work: Creating Excellence and Influencing Others at Work* by Dianna Booher.

Tim and his wife, Anna, serve families through www.timalba.com and parenting seminars near their home in the Dallas/Fort Worth area. They have three biological kids, three "bonus" kids (their kids' spouses), and a growing brood of grandchildren.